Public
Speaking
In An Instant

60 Ways to Stand Up and Be Heard

Public Speaking
In An Instant

- How to Prepare to Be Spontaneous
- Enliven Your Talks With Stories and Examples
- Make Your Audience Part of the Presentation

Keith Bailey and Karen Leland

CAREER
PRESS
Franklin Lakes, NJ

PUBLIC SPEAKING IN AN INSTANT
EDITED BY JODI BRANDON
TYPESET BY MICHAEL FITZGIBBON
COVER DESIGN BY HOWARD GROSSMAN/12E DESIGN
PRINTED IN THE U.S.A. BY BOOK-MART PRESS

To order this title, please call toll-free 1-800-CAREER-1 (NJ and Canada: 201-848-0310) to order using VISA or MasterCard, or for further information on books from Career Press.

**P CAREER
PRESS**

The Career Press, Inc., 3 Tice Road, PO Box 687,
Franklin Lakes, NJ 07417
www.careerpress.com

Library of Congress Cataloging-in-Publication Data
Leland, Karen.
    Public speaking in an instant : 60 ways to stand up and be heard
/ by Karen Leland and Keith Bailey.
        p. cm.
    Includes index.
        ISBN 978-1-60163-018-6
    1. Public speaking. I. Bailey, Keith, 1945– II. Title.
    PN4129.15L46 2009
    808.5'1--dc22

                                                    2008035820

β
Leland

*To the power of words and their ability to
teach, heal, and inspire.*
—Keith Bailey

*To Dewitt Jones for not only being a great speaker, but
always taking the time to help me be a better one.*
—Karen Leland

Acknowledgments

Many thanks to our agent, Matthew Carnicelli, and the folks at Career Press for their support of the In An Instant series. Much gratitude to our clients and all the trainers and speakers we have had the privilege of working with and learning from. Lastly, to our spouses, Deborah and Jon—our biggest cheerleaders.

Contents

Introduction

Public speaking, though often considered the domain of the professional lecturer, is more a part of our lives than we realize. It's the supervisor who leads a meeting for a group of four and the book author who gives a keynote speech at a conference of 4,000 people. It's the salesperson who stands in front of clients to promote a product and the trainer who conducts seminars for her colleagues. It's the best friend who toasts the groom at his wedding and the daughter who speaks of her mother's passing at the funeral.

Regardless of the form it takes, good public speaking is all about connecting with your audience—knowing what your message is and getting it across in a way that educates, entertains, motivates, or moves—sometimes all at once.

Over the past 25 years we have had the privilege of leading thousands of training seminars for companies around the world, giving hundreds of keynote speeches to conference attendees and training scores of people to be better presenters, trainers, and public speakers.

Public Speaking In An Instant

This book is a compilation of everything we have learned from our own experience, our clients, and the other professional speakers we have watched and admired over the years. We sincerely hope it helps you to make your next speech, presentation, training, or meeting more of what you want it to be.

Analyze Your Audience

At first glance your audience may appear to be a mass of undistinguished faces in a crowd, but delivering your message to individuals—and then crafting your presentation accordingly—is one of the secrets to good public speaking. An important first step in delivering a **knock your socks off** speech is to research who exactly you will be speaking to and what it is they need or want from you. You can do this by setting up a pre-event conference call with the meeting coordinator. The eight key questions to ask are:

1. What is the ratio of male to female attendees?

Consider how the makeup of the audience might alter your presentation. For example: If you are giving a talk on "Career Advancement in Information Technology" and your audience is three-quarters female, you might want to spend extra time discussing the specific challenges facing women in the industry.

2. What geographic regions are represented?

If your audience members hail from a wide geographic smorgasbord (say, from Iowa to India), you may need to tweak certain aspects of your presentation. For example: American colloquialisms and idioms (*catch some rays, go bananas, goofed up*) will be understood by anyone from the States, but could leave foreigners scratching their heads.

3. What percentage of the group is made up of front-line staff, mid-level managers, and/or executives or owners?

Addressing a group of bank presidents can be very different than talking to a group of bank tellers. Depending on the level of individuals you will be speaking to you should:

- Choose the specific concerns to be addressed.
- Customize the examples you use.
- Tailor the solutions you recommend.

4. How long have most of these people been with the company or in the industry?

Attendees who have been around for a long time—have seen, heard, and done it all—will feel talked down to if the information you present is too run of the mill. For example: If you are conducting a break-out session for a group of veteran salespeople with 20-plus years' experience in the industry, discussing how to overcome the fear of asking for the sale might be a bit below their current skill level. The more experienced the group, the harder you have to work at coming up with leading-edge information or a new, innovative way of presenting core information. On the other hand, if your audience is made up of mostly newbies, a good review of the fundamentals won't hurt.

5. What is the age range of the group and what is the average age?

If you talk about Mister Rogers and how he changed the face of children's television to a group of Baby Boomers, they will nod in recognition and probably smile remembering the good times they had watching him. The Generation X folks in the audience may vaguely know who you are talking about and say, "I've heard of him." But use this example with an assembly of Generation Y workers and blank stares will more than likely be their response. The examples you use, the experts you quote, and the humor you pepper your presentation with should all be age appropriate to your audience.

6. What are the biggest concerns facing the group right now?

Dig a little deeper to find out what current circumstances are impacting the group. For example: If you are speaking about "Technology's Impact on Inventory Control," your pre-conference call might reveal a big concern about job security and rampant downsizing within the industry. Integrating this aspect of technology's impact into your speech will help build rapport and credibility with your audience.

7. How big is the audience?

Although the size of the audience won't change the subject you speak about, it may affect the way you deliver your presentation. For example: If you are talking to a group of 20 people about "Time Management Tips for the Busy Executive" you could easily have the participants do a role-play exercise or take questions as you go along. But if your group is 2,000 people strong, these same strategies could be a logistical challenge to pull off.

8. What is the overall education level of the group?

Knowing if your audience are blue-collar workers with a high-school education or a bunch of high-powered Harvard MBAs will impact the vocabulary, examples, and illustrations you use.

Speaker Savvy: Only about one-third of U.S. high-school graduates obtain a college diploma, and less than 10 percent of those go onto earn a graduate degree.

Arrive Early

Whenever possible, arrive with enough time to mingle with your audience before you get up to present. Take note of the kinds of topics being discussed, the concerns being expressed, and the general mood of the group. If need be, this allows you to do a quick adjustment to your presentation style or content to better fit with the audience.

Create an Outline

If you like to sit and watch paint dry, then you're probably one of the few people who enjoys listening to a public speaker who reads his/her speech verbatim. Most audiences, however, find this delivery boring. The alternative—memorizing your speech, word perfect—is too daunting and difficult to be practical. The overall best solution is to come up with an outline.

An outline is a skeleton of your speech comprised of short sentences that cover the essential points you want to make. Rather than reading these notes aloud, you use them as reminders of what you want to say. An outline is only effective if you've practiced your speech. It's not a substitute for preparation.

The following example contains a few paragraphs from a prepared talk followed by a sample outline. Notice that the outline is written in large, bold type. This is so it can be easily seen and quickly comprehended from the podium during a talk.

Original Prepared Talk

Bad grammar and poor spelling are much more commonplace than you might imagine. In a recent survey, it was found that 4 out of 10 business e-mails contain mistakes that are noticed by the receiver. If you send business e-mails with poor spelling, you will lose credibility with your clients.

Part of the problem is that we tend to write the way we speak, and this doesn't always translate to a well-written message. I recommend reading every e-mail through before clicking the "send" button, so that you can catch (and change) anything that sounds awkward.

When you read an e-mail, the sensory cues of body language and tone of voice that you would get during a real live conversation are missing. Over the phone your tone of voice coveys whether you are happy, serious, upset, or joking. In an e-mail your words are in an emotional vacuum and can easily be misinterpreted by the reader.

Outline of the Prepared Talk

- **Bad grammar, poor spelling common**
- **4/10 contain mistakes**
- **Loss of credibility**
- **Writing and speaking different**
- **Read before sending**

- No sensory clues
- Emotional vacuum
- Misinterpreted

Depending on your preparation level and confidence, you may want to add a little more information to the outline. If you are a more seasoned speaker, you might want to whittle each point down to one or two words—just enough to give you the gist of the point you are going to make.

Exercise

In the space provided, please write out the details of one point from one presentation you are planning to give:

_____

_____

_____

_____

_____

_____

Now, take this description and turn it into a big, bold, bulleted outline, using only keywords to tip you off as to the points you want to cover:

-
-
-
-
-
-

Design Your Talk

There are two core methods for delivering a presentation: reading a verbatim speech and delivering your talk extemporaneously, which involves using notes as a guideline but speaking in a more natural and unrehearsed manner. Reading your speech, word for word, can be boring and is usually best left for talks in which every word needs to be measured carefully. For example: A political speech or the presentation of highly delicate or difficult information. Designing an extemporaneous talk is a five-step process that begins by capturing the key information you want to discuss and then whittling it down to a few brief notes that will act as prompts for your delivery.

Step 1: Decide on the key points you want to cover.

If, for example, you are delivering a talk called "Using E-Mail Effectively in the Workplace," your key points might be:

- Common e-mail writing mistakes
- When it's inappropriate to use e-mail
- Understanding privacy issues
- Techniques for creating e-mail rapport

Step 2: Develop sub-points for each key point.

Next, take each key point you have come up with and break it down into it's logical and necessary sub-points. For example:

The key point "Common e-mail writing mistakes" might be broken down into the following sub-points:

- Poor spelling and bad grammar
- Lack of greeting or sign off
- Unclear subject line
- Missing a clear request
- CCs to too many people

Step 3: Script each sub-point.

The next step is to write out a few words about what you want to say about each sub-point. For example:

Addressing "Poor spelling and bad grammar," you might write:

Bad grammar and poor spelling are much more commonplace than you might imagine. In a recent survey, it was found that 4 out of 10 business e-mails contain mistakes that are noticed by the receiver.

If you send business e-mails that include poor spelling you will lose credibility with your clients.

Step 4: Gather supporting evidence and visual aids.

As you script each sub-point, look for opportunities to give examples, present survey findings, and show graphs, tables, and other pertinent visual aids. For example: The scripted phrase "In a recent survey, it was found that 4 out of 10 business e-mails contain mistakes that are noticed by the receiver," lends itself to a slide showing a graph of the survey results.

Step 5: Refine and add interactivity.

Once you have completed steps 1 through 4, you will have the body of your presentation mapped out. The next step is to refine it by going over the draft and looking at the order in which you will present your material, the support material you have in place, and any rough spots that need clarification.

Lastly, if appropriate, look for opportunities to include your audience in the presentation. Is there anyplace where a role-play, a small group discussion, or an interactive exercise would be suitable? Two or three audience activities in a 60–90 minute presentation will improve the group's receptivity.

Speaker Savvy: *For your presentation to sound natural, you need to take the script and turn it into an outline of concise notes that you can quickly refer to when giving your speech.*

Exercise

Think about a presentation you have coming up or a speech you would like to deliver.

Write down five key points you want to cover.

1._____

2._____

3._____

4._____

5._____

Choose one key point from your list, and write down three sub-points you want to make.

1._____

2._____

3._____

Choose one of your sub-points, and script it here.

_____

_____

_____

_____

For this same sub-point script, note the visuals or support material you could use.

_____

_____

_____

_____

A Good Speech Is Like a Deli Sandwich

A well-designed talk is like a juicy deli sandwich: At the heart of it is the information you deliver (the meat), and at the beginning and end there is the introduction and conclusion (the rye bread). The idea is to make your "two slices" compelling and memorable.

As well as a good introduction, audiences like a conclusion that re-caps the main points you have covered. Don't end with a whimper. Add extra seasoning to your final slice by ending with a brief, pithy story, or an insightful or moving quote that is pertinent to what you have presented.

Prepare Your Introduction

Because nervousness and anxiety are usually at their greatest during the first few minutes of a presentation, it makes sense to prepare and practice a killer introduction. Well-put-together open-ings will achieve three things:

1. Lay Out a Road Map of Your Talk

Your audience will be more attentive to your message if they have an idea of the terrain ahead. By clearly stating the purpose of your presentation and then encapsulating the main areas of your talk, the participants knows what to expect. For example:

The purpose of the presentation: *"I am going to talk today about the stress that most of us experience at work, how it affects our mental and physical health, and some very practical ideas for what to do about it."*

The main ideas: *"Stress isn't new, but in the last 10 years stress levels have increased at an alarming rate. I will be talking about what has caused this increase and the role that technology and downsizing have played. I will also discuss the fallout, which includes higher health-care costs for organizations and more absenteeism. Lastly, we'll look at five ways that you can reduce your stress at work...."*

2. Establish Your Credibility

Your authority as a presenter is granted when your audience perceives you as competent in your delivery, and honest and accurate with your information. Your first few minutes on stage are a moment of truth when the group assesses these attributes and quickly decides what they think of you. Here are some of the signs audiences look for. Are you:

Still and centered?	Or	Moving around nervously?
Speaking clearly?	Or	Rushed and garbled?
Enthusiastic and high-toned?	Or	Subdued and monotone?
Organized?	Or	Muddled and confusing?
Making eye contact?	Or	Glossing over their faces?
Sticking to your message?	Or	Losing your point/focus?

You can also help establish your credibility by letting your audience know about your experience with and education in the topic. However, no matter what your qualifications, their first (and second) impressions will almost always outweigh your credentials.

3. Get the Audience Engaged

Besides establishing your credibility, you can use your introduction to begin to get the audience engaged in your talk by:

- Asking pertinent, closed-ended questions. Audiences like to feel included, and one fast way to accomplish this is to ask them their opinion on a relevant topic. Closed-ended questions are asked in such a way as to evoke a yes or no answer. For example:

  "How many of you have felt stressed about work—while lying in your bed at night?"

- Using audience members' names. Pick a person from the audience, and if he/she is not wearing a nametag that you can see, ask his/her name. Then give an example that illustrates a point from your introduction using the person you have chosen. For example:

  "Stress is not only emotional, it is physical, too. For example, let's say that Anne (audience member's name) was getting close to missing a deadline. What might she feel as the physical symptoms of stress?"

  Note that the question is being asked of the whole audience, not just of Anne, because this would put too much pressure on her to come up with answers. Anne's role is completely passive—you are simply using her in your example.

Be Ordinary

No matter how intelligent, qualified, and poised you are, you want your audience to know that you are, in many ways, just like them. Including a few personal facts in your introduction allows the audience to feel they know you a little better. For example:

"Sometimes I don't even realize how stressed I am. The other day I was making pancakes for my 11-year-old grandson, Angelo. As I stood in the kitchen mixing the ingredients he looked over and said, 'Boy, Grandpa, from the way you're beating that batter I'd say you were seriously stressed!'"

Grab Attention From the Get-Go

You may find this hard to believe, but your audience doesn't always start off paying a great deal of attention to what you're saying. Often they are still getting settled in their seats, finishing up a conversation with the person next to them, or fiddling with their iPhone. You have to snag their interest right from the get-go with an attention=grabbing statement or activity. Use the following three approaches to ensure that all eyes are on you right from the start.

1. Make a Dramatic Statement

Dramatic statements can be statistics or events that are surprising and/or thought-provoking. Let's say you were giving a speech to a group of corporate lawyers and you started with the following statement:

"Sixty-eight percent of U.S. employees who use e-mail at work have sent or received e-mail that could place their company at risk."

It's safe to say that statement would grab their attention.

Exercise

Consider a presentation you have coming up and determine several dramatic statements you could make at the beginning of your talk. You may want to do a little Web research and see what comes up that is recent and relevant. Write your statements here.

2. Quote an Industry Authority

A powerful opening quote, from an authority who is respected and known to your audience, is an excellent attention-getting option—especially if the authority has had recent media coverage. If you were giving a sales presentation to a software company, you might start by using a recent quote from their CEO:

"As your Chief Executive Officer said at last week's Software Developer's Conference in Las Vegas: The future of computing is in fruit-scented microchips."

Exercise

Consider a presentation you have coming up and determine an industry expert you could quote. Again, you may want to do a little research on the Web to see the latest and greatest from this person. Write the quotation here.

3. Ask a Key Question

Many professional speakers have found that by asking a direct and compelling question right up front they engage their audience's attention immediately. A few good types of questions to ask include:

"What If?" Questions

Ask your audience to consider what life would be like with or without something. For example, you're speaking to a small group of women business executives on the importance of taking vacations. Question: How would you feel if you were not able to take a vacation for two years?

Recent Findings Questions

Ask your audience to think about information that relates to them, but they may not know about. For example, you're speaking to a group of parents at the monthly PTA meeting about the Internet and it's impact on children. Question: Did you know that we have had 10 cases of Internet bullying in our school this last month?

"What About You?" Questions

Everyone is always interested in how things apply to them, so ask your audience a question about one of their favorite topics—themselves! For example: You're leading a brainstorming session within your department about how to rewrite the current customer service policy on returns. Question: What part of the returned items process are each of you most familiar with?

Exercise

Consider a presentation you have coming up and determine one type of key question you would like to ask to get the audience's attention.

Write the key question here.

_____

_____

Warm Up With Icebreakers

Icebreakers are designed to warm up your audience by getting them acquainted and comfortable with being in the room and with one another. They are especially useful if your audience hail from different places and do not know each other. Icebreakers are usually in the form of fun games that get people up and moving or improvisational exercises that have participants work together to solve a light-hearted problem. Here a just a few ideas to get you started:

Hands Up, Fingers Down

Use with small groups that you want to get to know each other.

Time needed: 5–15 minutes.

Each participant sits in a circle holding up both hands. One person begins by asking the group a personal, yes/no question, presented as a statement, such as "I like to bike ride." Each group member responds to the statement. If his/her answer is "no," he/she puts down one finger. Now there are 9 remaining. The next person presents another yes/no statement to the group and so on, until only one person is left in the group with a finger still up. The statements can be mundane, silly, or extraordinary—the point is that you never know about people. Sample statements include:

- "I own a dog."
- "My checkbook is always balanced."
- "I have been to Spain."
- "I speak a foreign language fluently."
- "I have been skydiving."
- "I once rode a camel."
- "I helped birth a cow."
- "I teach rock climbing in my spare time."

My Partner Is...

Use with small groups when you want everyone to have a chance to get to know each other.

Time needed: At least 20 minutes, depending on the size of the group.

Have your audience members pair up. One partner then interviews the other person for 2 minutes. When the time is up, the partners switch roles. Once finished the group reconvenes, and everyone has the opportunity to introduce their partner to the group at large and share what they learned.

A Mixed Bag

Use with any size audience. It works especially well with groups that are already familiar with each other.

Time needed: 10–20 minutes, depending on the size of the group.

Ask each member of the group to write down three "facts" about himself/herself. Two of them must be true and one of them a complete fabrication. Then ask everyone to circulate around the room showing their list to as many people as possible and having them guess which one is the fabrication. When the group reconvenes, ask for feedback on what was learned.

Desert Island

Use with any size audience to promote understanding and teamwork.

Time needed: 15–30 minutes.

Form groups of five people each. Instruct the groups to pretend that they are shipwrecked on a desert island and each person is allowed to bring three items with them. Ask each person to write down his/her items. Next have each member share the items he/she wrote down and have the group reach a consensus decision on which five, of the 15 total, would be the most important to have—making sure that everyone in the group has at least one item represented. Afterward, conduct a large group discussion on both what the group decided to bring, why they decided to bring it, and what was it like trying to come to consensus.

If I Were...

Use with any size group where you are looking to promote creativity and fun.

Time needed: At least 10 minutes, depending on the size of the group.

Tell the audience that they have a choice to be either:

- A vegetable.
- A historical figure.
- A household object.
- An animal.

Instruct each person to choose one specific thing they would be from this category. For example: a cabbage, Napoleon, a toaster, a ferret—and explain to the group why he/she would be that.

Spice Up Your Talk With Stories

Imagine sitting in a large auditorium at your company's annual "Technology and Customer Service" conference. The keynote speaker is a renowned expert in the field and the author of four books on the topic. How would you react to each of the following ways that the speaker could use to convey the message:

Paint the Big Picture

"It's important to understand that customers like to talk with human beings. And while technology can, in many ways, help us to better service our customers, it is critical to distinguish those times when a brief conversation might produce a better result for everyone."

How do you feel hearing this?

Invoke Research

"When you look at the studies, it's obvious that most customers like having the option of talking to a human being. In fact, research shows that most people dislike long voice-mail menus, advertising messages while waiting on hold, and pre-recorded incoming calls."

How do you feel hearing this?

Tell a Story

"The other day I was in my office when the phone rang. I picked it up and a woman answered saying, 'I have a very important message that you have to listen to.' A little taken aback, I said, 'okay,' and after a bit of clicking and whirring I found myself listening to a pre-recorded message saying something about the lease on my car. It took me a few seconds to realize that the voice on the other end was asking me questions that I was supposed to answer. Because the questions were not relevant to my situation, I didn't answer. I hung up! A few moments later the phone rang again. It was the same woman, saying, 'I have a very important message for you...." *This time I interrupted her.* 'I am not going to listen to that message again!'

'You have to,' she said.

'I'm not going to!' *I said.* 'The questions don't relate to my situation,' *I argued—digging in my heels.*

The woman was getting more and more exasperated with me. After a couple more back and forths there was silence.

Eventually the woman said, in a threatening tone, 'If you don't listen to the recording, you are going to have to talk with a real person!'

The point is that technology can, in many ways, help us to better service our customers, but it's important to distinguish those times when a brief conversation might produce a better result for everyone."

How do you feel hearing this?

Although all three methods (paint the big picture, invoke re-search, and tell a story) have their place in a winning presentation, nothing can give an otherwise-rudimentary talk a kick in the pants like a well-told tale. Storytelling is an important part of presenting because it speaks to everyone's common experience. As your audi-ence listens, each one can imagine himself/herself in a similar situ-ation to the one you're describing. Your point is hammered home because a story—like a parable—cuts across diverse viewpoints, attitudes, gender, and age.

Exercise

Think about a presentation that you have coming up. Review the current outline you have planned and select two or three important points from the script. Next come up with a story that you could use to illustrate each of these key points. Feel free to take a little poetic license to make it funnier or more dramatic.

Title of Presentation:

_____

Key Point #1:

_____

Corresponding Story:

_____

Key Point #2:

_____

Corresponding Story:

_____

Key Point #3:

_____

Corresponding Story:

_____

Speaker Savvy: The story doesn't have to be something that happened to you. It can be a story you heard from a colleague, something you read, or even a scene from a movie. Just be honest about where it comes from in the telling.

Compose a Great Story

Although facts and figures are an important part of your presentation, alone they offer a dull discourse. To spice up your speech, try pairing your statistics with a key ingredient: stories. Remember that not all stories are created equal. Use the following four tips to add fizz to your facts.

Tip: Expose yourself.

Don't be afraid to let the audience in on your personal foibles. People love to know (in detail) that you are as human, real, and fallible as they are. By unabashedly acknowledging your missteps, mistakes, and flaws, your story becomes more compelling.

Don't say: *"When I stood up to speak at the meeting, I was a bit concerned that people would disagree with me."*

Do say: *"When I stood up at the meeting, I was feeling really scared. I knew this group; they could easily turn into a pack of hungry dogs and I was afraid that they weren't going to like what I had to say."*

Tip: Delight in details.

The more precise and detailed your descriptions, the easier it will be for your audience to form a picture in their mind's eye. Once created, these pictures are remembered, long after the facts have faded.

Don't say: *"I was caught in the rainstorm and arrived at the client's office late."*

Do say: *"I was trying to get to my client's office when it started to storm. The rain was torrential—the sort that hurts when it hits your head. By the time I arrived, I looked like I had just stepped out of the shower, fully dressed. My pants were glued to my legs. Luckily I was wearing a waterproof watch, but I didn't need to look at that to know that I was already very late."*

Tip: Unfold the plot—quickly.

Stories should not be so long and drawn out that your tale loses momentum and your audience lose interest. As you prepare and rehearse your presentation, remove any words or phrases that are insignificant and would weigh down the plot line.

Don't say: *"With my new position came the rude awakening that I had to have a working knowledge of the gross domestic product, or GDP. The GDP is one of the many measures this country uses to calculate income and output. It's the sum of all the value that is added to the stages of production of goods and services produced here in the U.S. for a specific period of time. My job specifically involved government expenditures and any significant changes in the salaries of public servants. As you can imagine, it took me many months to fathom the inner workings of these economic measurements...."*

Do say: *"With my new position came the rude awakening that I had to have a working knowledge of the gross domestic product, or GDP. Roughly speaking, GDP is a broad measure of a country's economy. As you can imagine, it took me many months to fathom the inner workings of these economic measurements...."*

Tip: Sharpen your points.

Remember that a good story *always* illustrates a key point. Without a clear point, a story may be entertaining, but it will not educate, uplift, or enlighten your audience. As you look over the stories in your presentation, clarify for yourself the point you think each story makes. Then, prior to telling the story, clearly explain to the audience the point you are making. Once you have told your story, repeat its point one more time.

Don't say: *"I want to tell you a story about the time I was on a flight to New York and the airline failed to load everyone's luggage. As you can imagine, JFK was not a pretty place that night. There were two lost baggage agents on duty, each with a long line of bitter, complaining passengers. I noticed that one line was moving much faster than the other. I moved to the faster line and, when I got up to the window, I noticed an interesting attitude difference between the two agents. One was being polite, apologetic, and caring; the other abrasive, hard, and insensitive. Which line was moving faster? The one with the agent who appeared to be more compassionate and listening."*

Do say: *"There is a mistaken belief that giving good service is too time consuming to be practical. It just takes too long! Well, I disagree. Recently I was on a flight to New York.... Which line was moving faster? The one with the agent who appeared to be more compassionate and listening. The point is that the agent with the poor service attitude made upset customers more quarrelsome and each interaction took longer. The agent with a strong service attitude treated the customers as partners, and the line moved faster. The point? Good service does not necessarily take longer to deliver."*

Demonstrate Role-Plays

Audience involvement is a key component of an absorbing and stimulating presentation. Without it, listening to a speaker can be as exciting as watching rice cook. Role-plays are one of the most effective ways to get people participating and engaged. The downside is that when they are not set up correctly, they can misfire and turn an otherwise smooth-running presentation into pandemonium.

Here are the rules for setting up role-plays that guarantee success:

Rule 1: Make it clear that you are about to do a role-play.

Unless you're speaking at a convention of soothsayers, your audience will not be made up of mind readers who know where you are going and how you want to get there. Remember that they have never heard this presentation and don't know what comes next. By clearly explaining that they are about to do a role-play or exercise, the group knows what to expect and no confusion will ensue when you begin giving instructions. For example:

"In a few minutes we are going to do a role-play that will demonstrate the difference between helping and hindering a customer problem."

Rule 2: Demonstrate the role-play before asking your audience to do it.

For the most successful outcome, always demonstrate the activity from the front of the room, before asking the participants to try it themselves. This helps resolve any mysteries or misunderstandings and gives them a clear idea of what to do and how to do it. For example:

"First, I am going to do the role-play in the front of the room, so you can see how it works."

Rule 3: Don't ask for volunteers.

The words *can I have a volunteer?* can make even the most enthusiastic of attendees dive under the table for cover. Instead, casually pick a person from the audience (preferably one who seems more like an extrovert than introvert) and ask him/her to please come up and do the activity with you. Most people will accept your invitation. If they don't, say, "Okay; no problem," and pick someone else. For example:

For this I am going to need someone to help me. Jennifer, would you please come up and do this with me?"

Speaker Savvy: *Don't be fooled if the person you have called on at first frowns or puts forth reluctant rhetoric. Most people will moan a bit on principle, but, if you say nothing, they will most often get up out of their chair and make their way to the front of the room.*

Rule 4: Make the role-play scenario relate to the audience.

A role-play scenario that takes place in a retail store would work great with a group of department store sales assistants but fall flat on its face with an audience of accountants. For this reason, do your research and have some pre-planned role-play scenarios up your sleeve, or use the brainpower of the audience to spontaneously come up with a situation. For example:

"Jennifer, what is an example of a typical problem that a customer has in the course of your workday?"

Rule 5: Explain what will happen.

Methodically explain what you will be doing in the role-play every step of the way. For example:

"I'm going to have Jennifer play the part of the customer, and I'm going to play the part of the service provider. I am going to have the attitude that she is a pain.

"Jennifer, as the customer, I want you to respond as realistically as possible. React the way you would if you were a customer really dealing with an employee like me."

Rule 6: Debrief and thank the participant.

When the role-play is over, be sure to inquire about the participant's experience. For example:

"As the customer, how did it feel being treated that way?"

When done with the front-of-the-room debrief, thank the participant, ask the audience to thank the person by clapping, and invite the person to take his/her seat.

Set Up Successful Role Plays

Once you've done a demonstration of the upcoming role-play from the front of the room, the participants should be ready and raring to go. Even though your audience has just seen a sample of what the role-play should look like, you still need to walk them through the specific steps. A little bit of time spent on role-play setup will prevent confusion during the exercise.

To begin with, divide the group up into pairs. Give the attendees a few moments to do this. Be on the lookout for anyone who may need to move to another part of the room to find a free partner. Wait until everyone has been paired up and settled down before moving onto the next instruction.

Your next task is to have them choose which partner will go first, or which partner will play what role. Instead of the generic *"pick someone to go first"* or *"pick someone to play the customer,"* you can try making this fun by asking the pair to figure out who has the longest hair or shortest hair, or any other question that might distinguish them in a fun way. Be careful to stay away from anything that might seem offensive such as weight, age, and so on.

Once the participants have determined who is who, clearly explain which partner will be playing what role. For example:

"Longer-haired partner, please raise your hand. Thank you. You will play the part of the customer.

"Shorter-haired partner, please raise your hand. Thank you. You will play the part of the service provider."

Speaker Savvy: *Asking people to raise their hands lets you know that they know what part they are playing.*

Now that your audience knows who they are, the next step is to clearly outline what they will be doing. Specific instructions are key. For example:

"If you are playing the part of the service provider, please take a minute to describe a typical situation you encounter at work, where a customer with a problem calls you on the telephone. Don't start the role-play yet; just pick the scenario and explain it to your partner, who will be playing the customer. This will let your partner know what his or her role is."

Keep in mind that it usually takes a minute or two for people to come up with and explain a situation. Once you get the sense that everyone has a scenario ask:

"Is there anyone in the room who does not have a scenario?"

If any pair is stuck, take a moment to help them identify a scenario, or borrow one from another pair in the audience. Once everyone is set to go, proceed with the final instructions for each person. For example:

"Please raise your hand if you are the service provider. In a minute you will initiate the telephone conversation with your customer. Your job in this scenario is to have a negative attitude toward this person. Pretend that they are an interruption to your job and a real pain. Think of the way I treated Jennifer when she was up here doing the demonstration of the role-play with me.

"Now, please raise your hand if you are the customer. Your job is to respond, just the way you would if you were a customer and really being treated this way. Remember how Jennifer reacted during the role-play demonstration."

Speaker Savvy: *Having partners raise their hands again reduces any "identity" confusion prior to beginning the role-play. Also, referring to the demonstration as an example further minimizes any misunderstanding.*

"Does anyone have any questions? Okay. Please begin and keep going until I tell you to stop. You will have two minutes for this exercise."

Debrief Exercises and Role-Plays

Setting up a role-play or exercise in a way that clearly explains what to do is only half the game when it comes to exercise effectiveness. Just as important is debriefing the audience afterward.

The well-conducted debriefing process offers participants the opportunity to lock in what they have learned by reflecting on their realizations and hearing about other's experiences. The basic structure of an exercise debrief involves three different types of questions.

Big Picture Questions

These are general, open-ended questions that allow participants to take a bird's-eye view of their experience. Suggested questions include:

- "What was that exercise/role-play like for you?"
- "What did you notice playing the role of the____?"

- "How did you feel when you were playing the role of the____?"
- "What was easy or hard for you about that exercise?"

Meaning Questions

The next group of questions dives deeper into what the participants observed and are designed to help them narrow their larger experience down into specific learning and insights. Suggested questions include:

- "What did you learn from this exercise?"
- "What new insights did you have?"
- "Why is what you observed in this exercise important?"

Application Questions

This last group of questions helps participants to identify ways that they can apply their insights and experiences to their work-life and specific jobs. Suggested questions include:

- "How does what you observed relate to your job?"
- "How can you take what you learned back into your work-life?"
- "What specific changes could you make at work, based on what you learned?"

Speaker Savvy: The best trainers and presenters use a combination of the questions and a variety of methods (paired sharing, group dialogue, and small group feedback) to debrief role-plays and exercises.

Make Asking Questions Easy

The best speakers are those who not only welcome participation from the audience, but actively encourage it. One way to make it easy and safe for your group to speak up is to promote asking questions during the presentation, or at a designated Q&A session. Some easy ways to do this include:

- Pass out notepaper and ask the group to jot down any questions that arise during the speech.

Speaker Savvy: Ask people to stand up when they ask a question. It makes it easier for the audience to hear them and for you to identify who is asking.

- Set the stage from the start. Some speakers prefer to take questions as they arise; others will only entertain questions at the end of their presentation. To put your audience's minds at ease, let them know right from the start when you will be giving them a chance to pose their problems and solicit your answers.

- View all questions as valid. There are no stupid questions. Well, actually there are—but the point is to not view them as such or make the questioner feel like an idiot for asking them. The next time you get asked an off-the-wall question, think to yourself, "What is this person really asking?" Often, by paraphrasing the question back to the audience member, you discover the valid question hidden at the core.

- Validate each question asked. One way to encourage questions is to thank each and every person for the question he/she posed. You may want to say "good question" (if it was) or "I'm glad you asked that" (if you are) or "a lot people have that question" (if they do). If all else fails, thank the person for being willing to ask the question.

- Provide options. Because some people feel uncomfortable standing up and asking a question out loud, provide the option of passing a written question to you, or getting a note to you via the event coordinator.

- Answer to the whole audience. Although it's tempting to address just the questioner directly when you answer, deliver your response in the same way you would your speech—that is, give it to the whole group. This helps people to feel engaged and included.

Speaker Savvy: *As soon as you finish answering one question, immediately ask, "Who else has a question?" This keeps the momentum going.*

- Check for understanding. Once you are done answering a question, always check back with the person to make sure that he/she feels the question got answered. A simple "Did that answer your question?" will suffice. If he/she says no, ask him/her to specify what part of the question still needs to be answered. If he/she says yes, you can comfortably move onto the next inquiry. Doing this gives the audience the message that you really care about answering their questions.

Conduct a Q&A Session

Almost every formal speech features a Q&A (question and answer) session at the end of the presentation. Although venturing into the unknown realm of questions gives some speakers the shivers, it provides the audience with an opportunity to ask about specifics that were not covered in the session and/or to bring up topics that the talk triggered.

The questions you will get asked can range from insightful and pertinent to bizarre and unrelated. Regardless, your job is to answer them all, from the sublime to the silly, with the same professionalism, expertise, and aplomb. Though it's hard to prepare specific answers to questions you haven't yet heard, there are things you can do to succeed once the inquiry is before you.

Wait until the entire question is asked. Even if you think you know where the asker is heading, take a deep breath and wait for him/her to finish before giving your answer. Unfortunately, many people don't present their questions in a nice neat, package, and critical information may be tacked on at the end.

Repeat the question back. Doing this ensures that three things happen:

1. You make sure that everyone in the audience hears the question that was asked.
2. You make sure that you understood the question.
3. You buy yourself some time to come up with an answer!

Don't fake it. There will be times when you get asked a question that you don't understand, don't have time to deal with, or simply don't have an answer for. If this happens, resist the temptation to muscle your way through and fabricate a flimsy response. There is no shame in saying you can't answer a question. Instead, say something like:

"I'm sorry, I don't know the answer to that question."

"I'm sorry, I'm not quite sure what you are asking."

"I'm sorry, that is not a question I can answer in the time we have. Please see me at the end."

"I'm sorry, that is a bit out of my area of expertise."

Your audience will appreciate your honesty and trust you even more when you respond to questions you *can* answer.

Speaker Savvy: If you have a question you think would be better answered by your audience, by all means ask them for their input.

Shortcut rambling questions. If the questioner rambles on and on, don't be afraid to gently interrupt and say, "I think I understand what you are asking, and I can help shed some light on this." Then answer the question (or statement) with a very specific and definitive response that leaves little room for ambiguity.

Anticipate hot issues. Prior to presenting your talk, come up with a short list of likely questions and spend some time preparing to answer them. If your subject is particularly provocative, practice having a trusted friend or colleague ask you a few *questions from hell.* Even if nobody asks them, knowing that you are ready to answer them will boost your confidence level.

Speaker Savvy: Just in case you're faced with a group that is slow to ask questions, have a few of your own prepared. Simply say, "One question I get asked a lot is…"

Sum it up. As the Q&A session comes to and end, take a minute or two to summarize your talk, thank the group for their participation, or wrap up the session before concluding. Don't take the last question, say "thank you," and walk off the stage.

Make Your PowerPoint Powerful

If you've ever sat through a presentation by a boring speaker armed with a million slides, you know that *death by PowerPoint* is not a pretty sight. Poorly used visuals are counterproductive because the audience stops listening long before the show is over. Use the following do's and don'ts to bring your next PowerPoint presentation to life.

Public Speaking In An Instant

Do's:	Don'ts:
Use slides to augment the clarity and color of your talk.	Hide behind your slides and expect them to replace you in the starring role.
Limit each slide to a few lines of text.	Overload your slides with so much information that they resemble a newspaper.
Have simple transitions from one slide to another or from bullet point to bullet point.	Use spiraling, zooming, over-the-top-transitions.
Create slides that illustrate the key points you want to make.	Turn your slides into a transcript of your talk.
Leave slides on the screen long enough for people to read and make notes.	Whiz through each slide at the speed of light.
Use a remote slide changer that attaches to your computer.	Spend time fiddling with your mouse instead of looking at your audience.
Design a limited, uncomplicated, and consistent color scheme for your slide show.	Use every color recognized by the human eye.
Present your slides in a forward-moving, logical, and easy-to-follow order.	Dart back and forth between various slides in the front and back.
Distribute handouts of your slides before the presentation.	Assume that the audience will not want handouts and end up having to supply them later.
Complement your text with graphics and clip art.	Overwhelm your message with visual distractions.
Use a large, sans serif font (30 points or larger).	Use a typeface so small you have to supply your audience with binoculars.
Ensure that text stands out against the background by using high contrast colors (for example, dark blue and white).	Use color combinations (for example, light blue with light green) that will get lost when projected in a large room.
Face, speak, and direct your attention to your audience.	Face and focus on your slides.

Be Facile With a Flip Chart

Despite the proliferation of PowerPoint presentations, the good old-fashioned flip chart remains a staple in boardroom meetings, classroom training, and convention breakout sessions. Even if you plan on taking a high-tech approach at your next public speaking event, consider having a flip chart available just in case. A few advantages of the humble flip chart include:

- Flip charts are totally low-tech and require no electricity, lightbulbs, or extension cords.
- Flip charts are relatively inexpensive and plentiful. Every hotel, office supply store, and convention center has them.
- Flip charts support spontaneity. If a hot discussion ensues and you want to capture your audience's comments, you can—right on the spot.

Use the following do's and don'ts to make the most of your flip chart:

Do's:	Don'ts:
Prepare diagrams ahead of time by pre-drawing them on the flip chart.	Make your audience wait while you hastily sketch.
Speaker Savvy: If you don't have time to do the diagrams ahead of time, or need to draw them as the discussion occurs, outline your diagram lightly in pencil on the page, so you have an outline to follow.	
Leave a blank page between each pre-written sheet for comments, questions, exercises, and so on.	Leave the only blank pages at the back, forcing you to flip to the end to find a place to write.

Public Speaking In An Instant

Do:	Don't:
Create a summary on the last page of your flip chart that highlights the key points you made during your presentation.	Flip through each page of the presentation to go over what you covered.
Make your first page a title page that states the subject of your talk, offers a warm welcome to the participants, and/or contains your name.	Make the initial information from your session the first page. (This will distract your audience.)
Leave plenty of space between key points on a page so that you have room to write comments from the audience.	Jam a page so full of text with pre-written points that there is no room to spontaneously add text.
Write in big letters (approximately 3 inches tall) so that everyone in the room can read what you have written.	Write in all capital letters, which are weary on the audience's eyes.
Use a variety of colored markers. For text and large graphics, dark colors such as black, dark blue, and green work best. Brighter colors such as red and purple work for highlighting various aspects of what you have written or to make smaller diagrams stand out.	Use yellow, pink, or orange, as they are difficult colors for an audience to see.
Stand to the side of the flip chart after you have written an item down so that your audience can see what you have put up.	Keep you back to the audience the whole time while you write down their comments during a group discussion.
Invest in special flip-chart markers that won't bleed through the sheet.	Use regular markers, which have a stronger smell and tend to bleed through.
Look for flip-chart stands that have top clamps to secure the pad in place.	Use pads that just lean against the stand. They are unsteady and can fall over easily.

Speaker Savvy: Use pads that have grid lines on them to help you draw text and graphics neater and straighter.

Evaluate Your Presentation

In your own mind, you might see yourself as a sort of public speaking genius, a master of the medium, top of the heap. Others may have even told you how your talk rocked their world. However, everyone (and we do mean everyone) is subject to the pitfalls and hazards that can leave a presentation far from perfect. To keep improving, use the following questionnaire to evaluate your public speaking skills on a regular basis.

Part 1: Audience Reaction—During the Presentation

Question	Yes	No
1. Did the audience act interested and engaged by nodding, smiling, answering questions, taking notes, etc.?		
2. Did the majority stay until the end of my presentation?		
3. Did the audience maintain eye contact with me instead of fussing with papers or PDAs, or talking to the person next to them?		
4. Did the audience laugh in suitable spots and in general react appropriately to what I was discussing?		

5. Did the audience participate wholeheartedly in any role-plays or exercises I set up?		
6. Did the audience ask questions?		

Part 2: Audience Response—Immediately After the Presentation

Question	Yes	No
7. Did people come up to me with praise, questions, or comments?		
8. Did people ask for more information about my products and services, my company, and me?		
9. Did people take my handouts with them when they left the room?		
10. Did people request a copy of my slides?		
11. Overall, were the written evaluations positive?		

Part 3: General Feedback—Post-presentation

Question	Yes	No
12. Have I received e-mails or calls requesting information on my services?		
13. Have I received written compliments or calls about my presentation?		
14. Have I been invited to speak at other events?		
15. Have the media contacted me for interviews?		
16. Have the event organizers expressed satisfaction with my presentation?		

Part 4: Self-Evaluation

Question	Yes	No
17. Did I tell stories that added value to my talk?		
18. Was my take on the topic a good fit for this audience?		
19. Did I grab the audience's attention right from the start?		
20. Was the presentation logically organized and easy for the audience to follow?		
21. Did my visual aids add to my message?		
22. Did I have the right amount of pertinent data and statistics for this group?		
23. Was there some originality in either my information or the way I presented the topic?		
24. Did I have a strong ending to my presentation?		
25. Did I integrate enough examples of this group's needs, concerns, and issues?		
26. Did I pace my presentation so that I finished comfortably in the allotted time?		

SCORING

For each **yes** answer, give yourself 1 point. Add together your total number of points and review the guide that follows to see how you fared!

0–7 Points

Your presentation skills could use a bit of brush-up work. Though you may know your stuff inside and out, your ability to get it across to an audience needs some fine-tuning. Consider videotaping your next presentation so you can see, from a more objective point of view, what you are doing well and what needs improvement. Alternatively, you could have a friend or mentor sit in on your next presentation and give you an honest critique.

8–17 Points

You seem to have a solid grasp on the basics of public speaking and should build on your strengths. Several ways you can improve your presentation include: listening to other speakers and learning from what they are doing right; taking a public speaking workshop; reading a book (such as this one) on presentations; and taking some time before your next speech to work on your talk and practice your delivery.

18–26 Points

Congratulations! Your speech was a hit by all measures—yours and others! Don't rest on your laurels. Instead, continue to improve your professional presentation skills by moving your talk and delivery to the next level by:

- Speaking for bigger audiences.
- Adding more unique content and/or exercises to your presentation.
- Searching out and trying new presentation techniques.
- Consulting with a professional speaking coach.

Minimize Pre-presentation Fear

The popular comedian Jerry Seinfeld once made a joke about the well-known statistic that more people are afraid of public speaking than of death. Seinfeld noted that, if the numbers were accurate, people were five times more likely to desire being in the casket, than giving the eulogy!

All kidding aside, it is a fact that many people become anxious at the thought of having to talk in public. Often, the greatest degree of stress and stage fright happens in the 15 minutes prior to the curtain going up. Typical physical symptoms include:

- A galloping heartbeat
- Sweaty palms
- Nausea
- Shaking knees and/or hands
- Dry mouth
- The irrepressible urge to cough

If any of these symptoms sound familiar, implementing the following strategies can help you reduce your quaking-in-your-boots behavior:

Thoroughly prepare the first 10 minutes of your presentation. Because the first few minutes of a presentation are the scariest and most nerve-racking, having the beginning of your speech down cold will help you make it through. After this short period of time, most anxiety dissipates and you begin to get more comfortable and familiar with your audience.

Come up with worst-case scenarios. The day of the event, sit down and write out a list of the worst things you think could happen in your speech. Don't edit yourself. Simply write down whatever comes to mind, such as:

> *I would forget what to say.*
>
> *I would run off the stage crying.*
>
> *I would get hopelessly confused.*
>
> *The audience would get up and leave.*
>
> *The audience would boo and hiss.*
>
> *I could say something **really** stupid.*
>
> *The audience will be bored.*

Once you have your list, ask yourself which of these (if any) are likely to happen. If you do come up with one or two, figure out a strategy for dealing with them. For example: The potential problem of *forgetting what to say* could be resolved by keeping a cheat sheet with your speech outline on the podium in front of you. If you get stuck, take a sneak peak at the paper and get back on track.

Arrive early. Rather than rushing in at the last moment, plan on arriving early so you can spend some time schmoozing with the audience before you step up onto the stage. Finding out firsthand that they are not out to get you and are interested in what you have to say will go a long way to nixing your nervousness.

Notice your sensations. A lot of the anxiety you experience before a talk manifests itself as physical sensations within your body. Luckily, these intense feelings are usually not noticeable to anyone else. Rather than trying to push them aside and pretend they don't exist, take a quiet moment to feel what you are feeling as fully as possible. Breathe deeply and give them a bit of internal room. This might seem counterintuitive, but often, when you stop resisting uncomfortable feelings and face them down, they become softer rather than stronger.

Focus on your purpose. Instead of putting all your attention on how nervous you feel, think about the contribution you plan on making to your audience. It's not an accident that **you** are the one giving **this** speech to **these** people on **this** day!

Know 10 Times More

The least nervous speakers are the most confident ones. By only speaking on subjects that you really know and feel comfortable with, you avoid the fear of being "found out" as less knowledgeable than you should be.

Stand Down Stage Fright

For some people, no matter what precautions or preparations they have taken to minimize their anxiety before speaking in public, stage fright grabs hold of them—mid-delivery. If you're a member of that group, use the following tips to overcome the shakes during your speech:

Take a moment to "arrive." Many speakers are in such a hurry to get started that they never really land and take in the full scene before them. Instead, look out at your audience, take a couple of good deep breaths, and then start speaking. This whole process only takes a few seconds, but it sets you on the right track from the start.

Focus on the audience. Paying too much attention to your own thought process while standing on stage is undermining. If you find yourself thinking, *They don't like me, They don't look happy,* or *I sound terrible,* switch the focus of your attention to your audience. Placing your awareness out into the audience will force you to be present with them and pull your focus away from your *I'm nervous* inner dialogue.

Keep a balanced posture. If you are standing, distribute your weight evenly on both feet and avoid nervously rocking back and forth. If you are seated, sit toward the front of the chair and lean forward. Both of these postures increase your energy level and will physically make you feel more confident.

Trust your audience. If something does go wrong, your audience will be more understanding and patient if you don't fall apart, but instead maintain a relaxed decorum. For example, if you lose your place in your notes, simply stop talking and take a few moments to review them. If you get confused and deliver something incorrectly, say to your audience (without drama), "I'm sorry—that was incorrect. What I meant to say was…." Your audience expects you to be professional, not perfect.

Use a lectern. If you are concerned about shaking hands and wobbly knees, a lectern can be useful. You can lean on it if your legs turn to jelly, place your notes on it so that no one can see your hands shaking, and keep a glass of water handy if dry mouth hits.

Don't "try" to be a certain type of speaker. Some speakers add additional stress and pressure to their onstage time by trying to look and sound like a lecturer they admire. Although you can always borrow bits and pieces of speaking savvy from other presenters, the best strategy is to be yourself. If you're naturally funny, great—go for it. If, on the other hand, you're more the serious stories type, give yourself a break and build your talk on your unique talents.

Let Your Clothes Speak

Imagine going to see a speech by an author you have long admired but never seen in person. He walks on to the stage wearing a tacky pair of worn khaki slacks and a casual shirt with a stain on the collar, and a hairstyle that has not changed since 1943. *Who is this shabbily dressed shlub?* you think. *Certainly not my beloved author!*

Although you are still dazzled by his brilliant prose, his choice in clothing has left you disappointed and distracted. Like it or not, the clothes you choose when you speak can either hinder or help your credibility. To make the best first impression:

Wear fabrics that don't wrinkle. A sharp navy linen skirt suit with a smooth silk blouse underneath might look smart when your getting dressed at 9 a.m. but, by the time your lunchtime speech rolls around, your once-crisp ensemble will be a mass of creases. Look for fabrics that travel well and retain their freshness, even after a few hours of riding in a taxi or sitting in a chair.

Speaker Savvy: Remove your jacket while driving to avoid those unflattering diagonal folds caused by a seat belt. Also, steer clear of anything with linen and 100-percent cotton, and instead go for clothes that contain Lycra or wool blends.

Find a fabulous fit. What impression do the following create? Gaping buttons on a too-tight blouse; stomach spillage over the top of trousers; and a shirt collar that is choking the living daylights out of its occupant? Ill-fitting clothing leaves your audience with the impression that you don't care enough to dress well, are unable to dress well, or don't know the difference! In any case, clothes that are too tight (or too loose, for the matter) hurt your professional presentation.

Speaker Savvy: If you're big on gesturing, make sure you can easily raise your hands above your head and put them out to your sides without stress or strain.

Dress slightly better than your audience. While still taking into consideration the time, place, and purpose of the event, go slightly upscale in how you dress compared to your audience. For example: For many business conferences that take place in the islands, Hawaiian style shirts are the outfit du jour. If you are the speaker, by all means wear one, but make it a fancy silk shirt featuring a classy mix of pineapples and palm trees—not a common cotton one with half-naked hula girls plastered all over.

Enhance your message with what you wear. The clothes you wear should support, not conflict with, the ideas you are trying to impart. For example: If you are a Gold Medal long-distance runner talking to a group of salespeople on how to set and achieve goals, you would probably not show up for your speech in running shoes and shorts, but rather a suit and tie. The clothes you wear are not meant to be a fashion statement (unless, of course, you are speaking to a group of graduates from a fashion institute), but rather congruent with your audience and your message. Understanding the style of your audience will help you to determine what outfits will pack the most positive punch. Are they sporty, sophisticated, conservative, or creative? Dressing in the direction of your listeners helps to create instant rapport.

Dress the Part

You are scheduled to present a short speech to the CEO and his top talent before the morning round of golf, conduct a 100-person breakout session after lunch, and give the keynote presentation to the entire conference at the formal dinner that evening. The question is: What do you wear? Different situations and venues require diverse styles of dress. The key is to be appropriate. Some of the fashion factors to take into consideration when choosing your clothing include:

- **The audience.** Is this a group of seasoned senior executives or a gathering of Generation Y college graduates?
- **The location.** The dress code for a conference on the island of Maui is distinctly different from one that takes place in mid-town Manhattan.

- **The occasion.** Your attire for a toast at a wedding is 180 degrees different than your sartorial choices for a luncheon keynote at a company golf outing.

One easy way to decide what to wear for any public speaking engagement is to pay attention to the stated dress code for that event and attire accordingly. Knowing the following categories will help you avoid ending up in the awkward position of being over- or underdressed:

Sportswear: Many sports (such as golf and tennis) have stringent dress codes and require shirts with collars, long pants, particular shoes, and so forth. If you are speaking in the clubhouse, call ahead for the particulars.

Casual: This is all over the map these days, but broadly translated it means no sleeves, collars, or jackets required. You are usually safe with nicer jeans (no rips), cotton slacks, tasteful T-shirts, sleeveless tops, longer shorts, and snazzy sandals (leave the flip-flops at home).

Speaker Savvy: One sub-category of casual wear is super-duper casual or fun wear. Think a beach party or barbeque here. Shorts, sleeveless tops, shorter skirts, casual open-toe sandals, and swimsuits are the order of the day. However, keep in mind that, as the speaker, you probably don't want to be giving your talk in a tank top and flips-flops.

Business Casual: In general, this means a tie is not required but a shirt with a collar is. Slacks, blouses, and not-too-short skirts are the staple of this category. Sorry, but jeans are out.

Semi-Formal: For men, this indicates a relatively conservative business suit and tie with no overly loud colors or patterns. For women, a business suit (skirt or pants) with closed-toe shoes.

Cocktail: For women, this is the occasion that the Little Black Dress (LBD) was invented for. Dresses can be slightly shorter and worn with open-toe shoes. Slacks, if worn, should be of a nicer fabric such as satin, silk, velvet, or a blend.

Men should wear business attire with a jacket and tie.

Formal: A dark suit and conservative tie for men and elegant dresses or formal pant suits for women. Women will usually wear closed-toe shoes, but high-heeled, open-toe shoes may be acceptable.

Black Tie: The beauty of dressing for a black tie event is its simplicity. For men—a tuxedo; for women—a long dress.

White Tie: In the event that you have reached that pinnacle of professional success where you are asked to speak at or attend an official government function, white tie may be required. On these occasions, men wear long white or black tailcoats with matching trousers, and women wear long formal gowns (often with gloves).

Choose Your Color Carefully

A dazzling red suit, a bright blue tie, a sleek black dress—all say something to the people watching about the person wearing them. There is no doubt that the colors you choose to dress in when making a presentation communicate a message to your audience. According to color experts, different colors have different meanings and impact.

Your Key to Colors

	Meaning/Impact	Downside
Black	Power, authority, stylish, thinning	Hard to see when standing in front of dark backgrounds
White	Fresh, light, crisp	Shows dirt easily
Gray	Intellect, knowledge, wisdom	Very conservative when worn as a suit
Red	Emotion, intensity, attention-grabbing	Can be overpowering when worn in quantity
Pink	Approachable, compassionate	Tends to make certain complexions look washed out
Blue	Calm, peace, serenity	In the wrong shade can read as cold
Green	Earthy, natural, nurturing	Some shades can look institutional
Yellow	Sunny, optimistic, bright	Can be hard on the eye and overpowering
Purple	Luxury, wealth, sophistication	Can be wearing on the eyes over a long period of time
Brown	Solid, reliable, stable	Reads as dull on some people

To determine what color to wear for a particular speaking engagement consider the following:

1. What colors look best on me? Begin by assessing the color of your skin tone, eyes, and hair. For example: A rust brown jacket that picks up your auburn hair; a navy blue suit that matches the color of your eyes' or a peach blouse that blends perfectly with your creamy complexion. In general, repeating the color of your skin, hair, and eyes in your clothing is a good way to go.

2. What type of group am I presenting to? Is the audience a conservative group of bankers or a smoking hot assembly of ad executives? The more fashion-oriented and glamorous your listeners, the more hip and happening your color combinations can be.

Basic Black

Brenda Kinsel, a nationally recognized image consultant and author of *In The Dressing Room With Brenda* (Wildcat Canyon Press, 2001) says black may be a business basic, but, when it comes to public speaking, ought not to stand alone.

"I really feel that unless you are mixing a lot of interesting textures together (such as a shiny black jacket with matte black pants and a black patent leather belt) black is too drab," says Kinsel. She feels that part of the speaker's job is to stand out by being more put together and polished than anyone in the room. "If you really want to wear black, add a pop of brighter color—such as lime green, coral yellow, or red in your tie, scarf, or jacket. You can also incorporate a softer shade of lilac, aqua, or blue green," says Kinsel.

Infuse Your Voice With Inflection

If you have ever sat through a presentation where the speaker drones on and on, you know the pain of having to listen to a tone of voice with too little inflection in it.

Inflection is the variation in pitch (the highs and lows) of your voice. Used well, it can accentuate certain words, add meaning and emphasis to what you are saying, and compel an audience to listen. Without it, you run the risk of coming across with a tedious sameness that can kill even the most interesting of topics.

Why, then, do so many orators—who are otherwise good conversationalists—seem to fall into the rut of mechanical and monotone speaking as soon as they step in front of the room? One simple reason is that most people fail to adjust their tone for the stage. Instead they use their everyday voice, which, given the distance between the presenter and the audience, renders the common non-dramatic conversational tone, ineffective.

The solution, as one participant in a workshop called it, is to learn to be multi-tone. In other words, rev up the drama in your speaking voice by adding excitement at certain places in your presentation and emphasis on particular phrases. If you're concerned that these types of vocal gymnastics might make you sound like a disc jockey, fear not—Your audience will appreciate your efforts and reward you with the gift of their attention.

Exercise

If you can get your hands on a tape recorder, tape yourself doing this exercise, so you can play back the recording and hear how you sound. If not, try doing the exercise with a friend or colleague so you can get his/her feedback. Alternatively, you can always do these exercises out loud by yourself.

Say the following sentence aloud, but don't alter your pitch as you speak and try to sound as monotone as possible.

"People tell me my public speaking is interesting and educational."

What adjectives (for example, dull, uninteresting, boring) would you use to describe how you sound? Are you filled with enthusiasm by what you just said?

Now go to the other end of the spectrum and say the following sentence, but with an overabundance of inflection. Think of that really obnoxious DJ on the AM radio station. Really overdo it.

"People tell me my public speaking is interesting and educational."

What adjectives (for example, fake, scary, irritating) would you use to describe how you sound this time? Are you convinced by what you said?

Lastly, adjust your inflection so that it sits comfortably between monotone and DJ. Repeat the phrase below, adding inflection to those words that you want to accentuate.

"People tell me my public speaking is interesting and educational."

What adjectives (for example, interesting, credible, comfortable) would you use to describe how you sound? Are you filled with confidence by what you just said?

Adjust Your Volume

Your voice not only transmits your message to your audience—it also transmits your energy level. For example: Think of Charlton Heston's deep, loud, booming voice in the movie *The Ten Commandments*. The impact would be very different if he spoke in the soft tones of a church mouse and three octaves higher! The goal is to use your volume purposefully.

Can You Hear Me Now?

Although a soft voice can be calming and pleasant, prolonged exposure can make an audience strain to hear or sleepy, and may send the wrong message. For example: Imagine the following sentence said in a quiet and unassuming tone:

"I've just gotten word from the hotel manager that a tornado is headed toward the hotel and we all need to evacuate the room immediately."

Stop Shouting!

On the other end of the spectrum is a presenter who bellows his entire speech, causing the group to become tense, irritated, and stressed. For example: Imagine the result if the speaker shouted at the top of his or her lungs about the tornado about to touch down.

Either way, ongoing volume (too loud or too soft) is ineffective. The key is to adjust your volume as needed to emphasize a point, catch the audience's attention, and add dramatic tension to your presentation. For example: Telling a story where your voice gets louder and more intense as the story unfolds draws your audience in. The drama can be further intensified by then lowering your voice to deliver the punch line.

Speaker Savvy: Your normal speaking volume is affected by room acoustics and the microphone system you are using. Plan on practicing in the room ahead of time and adjusting your volume until you can be heard all the way in the back and both sides of the room.

Exercise

Sound is made as air is forced from your lungs through your voice box; the greater the volume of air, the louder you sound. If you're having problems with speaking too softly, chances are you are forcing the air from your chest—rather than from your abdomen. To increase your volume, try the following:

Step 1: Place your hands on your chest and speak as if you were in front of an audience. Notice how your lungs are doing most of the work to make the sound. This type of shallow chest breathing does not have the power to create deep volume and can tire you out during a long speech.

Step 2: Next, place your hands on your diaphragm, located just below your lungs. Take a few deep breaths in and out, so that you feel your diaphragm expand and contract easily. Take one last deep diaphragmatic breath and speak as if you were in front of an audience. Notice how you have more power behind your voice. This type of deep breathing gives you a richer, deeper sound and will sustain you during a long speech.

Talk Fast and Slow

Just as the pitch of your voice can be deliberately varied for different effects, so can the rate at which you speak. For example: In his book *The Art of Public Speaking* (McGraw Hill Higher Education, 2003), author Stephen Lucas points out that Martin Luther King's famous "I Have a Dream" speech begins at a gentle 92 words per minute, and finishes up at a galloping 145 words per minute, bringing the crowd to its feet!

Getting your rate of speech just right is a matter of paying attention and practice. If you find yourself speaking too fast, it's usually due to nervousness and anxiety. Rushing through your presentation robs your audience of vocal variations—and the silent pauses—that help pull them into your presentation. Speaking too slowly, on the other hand, can put your audience to sleep!

According to research by Carver, Johnson & Friedman, the average person talks at a rate of about 125–175 words per minute, but listens at a rate of up to 450 words per minute, meaning that your audience can process information much faster than you can deliver it. So in the spaces in-between, you run the risk of being tuned out. One way to counter this listening time warp is to plan out the places in your speech, where you intentionally want to speed up and slow down.

First, take out the written outline of a presentation you plan to deliver. Find two or three places within the speech where it would add dramatic effect or impact to speed up, and mark them on your script. Next, find two or three places where it would be beneficial to slow down; mark those also. Lastly, locate several places in the speech where a pause could be strategically used to allow your point to penetrate.

Once you have made your choices, tape record yourself practicing the presentation with all the rate of speech changes you've made. Play the tape back and notice what was effective and what could still use improvement. Make the necessary adjustments, do one more run-through, and you're good to go in front of a live audience.

Practice Makes Perfect

Whether you're a speed demon who rushes through all your presentations or a take-it-slow speaker, if you want to stretch your rate of speech skills, try the following exercise:

Pick a poem, story, essay, or part of a text you know well and like. Tape record yourself reading through the piece quickly the first time and slowly the second. Play the tape back and note the impact each rate of speech has on you as the listener. Finally, record yourself reading the passage one last time, with a mix of speeds throughout. When you play the tape back, make a note of what speeds work well in which parts. Keep adjusting your reading until you know what combinations add the most impact to the piece.

Gesture Naturally

According to research, at least half (55 percent) of the impact and impression you make as a speaker comes from your body language. Using powerful body language makes you a more potent speaker and supports the message you are trying to get across. Consider the following:

- The stereotypical late-night TV car dealer shouting into the camera about the upcoming weekend super sale while his arms flail about as if a bi-polar puppeteer is controlling them, and his face contorts as if in a wind tunnel.

- The lecture by a scientist who stares—deer-in-headlights style—into the camera, his body motionless.

Neither of these approaches works because neither looks natural. The question is: How do you "do" natural body language when you're standing in front of an audience? The answer is to learn to gesture consciously—rather than unconsciously—when you speak. Here are a few tips:

Do's	Dont's
Vary the gestures you use, to fit the points you are making. Go through your speech and see where you might add emphasis.	Use the same hand gesture over and over. It gets boring, loses its impact, and ultimately means you are moving without thinking.
Pepper your presentation with gestures that initiate from the shoulders and elbows. These are better seen and have a bigger impact.	Have all your gestures come from the hands and wrists. These can be too insignificant, especially in front of a large audience.
Let your arms fall to your sides sometimes, to make the power of your gestures even more potent.	Rely on your memory for where to add gestures and movement.
Make specific notes in your outline about where you move and gesture.	Overdo it by using a gesture to make every point.
Use your whole arm, or both arms, to make a point.	Use pointed-finger or closed-fist gestures. (They can be taken as offensive.)

Size Matters

The relatively small hand gestures you use in everyday conversation probably won't be big enough to make an impact on a large audience. Always scale your gestures up or down to fit the size group you are speaking to.

Practice Standing Still

More often than not, nervous energy is what causes speakers to move mechanically. Without thinking, you might pace back and forth, or stare straight ahead never looking from side to side, or continually move your hands in a karate chop motion. Regardless, the first—and most difficult—lesson to learn is being able to speak without moving your body at all. If this sounds counterintuitive to all the advice you have ever read (including in this book), fear not. You can only really move with naturalness and ease when you know how to stand still first. To learn how to move with purpose instead of pace with nervousness, try the following exercise.

Exercise

Stand in front of a mirror (full length if possible) and make eye contact. Begin delivering your talk to the person in the mirror. For obvious reasons, it's a good idea to do this in private, rather than in public. As you speak to your own reflection, force yourself to stay still. Keep your arms pinned to your sides, your feet glued to the floor, and your torso facing front. Notice how you *really* want to move. Resist the urge. Persist until you can deliver your speech (or even a small part of it) without moving. Congratulations!

Now it's time to practice on a real person. Ask a family member or friend if he/she is willing to sit down and simply watch, while you stand up and deliver your talk—or part of it—to him/her. Do you feel like you want to move? Don't—just keep on talking. At first this may seem like a difficult (if not impossible) task. Eventually, though, with a little patience, you will be able to make eye contact and focus on what you are saying—without any distracting movement. *Bravissimo!*

Having strengthened your ability not to move, now it's time to go back to the mirror and add some natural movements. Begin the same way you did before—without moving. Get comfortable with the person who is reflected back at you. After a few minutes of delivering your talk, when it feels right, allow yourself to move your arms. Don't overdo it—just simple movements that emphasize a point or illustrate your words. Next look from side to side as if focusing on other audience members. Finally, walk toward the mirror, away from it, to the left, and to the right. Keep going until you have delivered your entire talk, in the mirror, with purposeful movement.

If you do this exercise several times, you will begin to get an internal feel for which movements are natural and which area result of nervousness. Knowing this will allow you to stop when you are acting anxiously, stand still for a moment and then continue on with deliberate and purposeful movements.

Establish Eye Contact

During the era of the 8mm movie camera, Kodak sponsored a short instructional film on how to shoot a home movie. One of their first warnings to newbie moviemakers was: "Don't Hose-pipe!" Hosepiping, as they explained, was continually moving the camera and never stopping to focus on any one thing.

Novice (or nervous) speakers are prone to do the same thing when it comes to eye contact. For example, you stand before your audience and deliver your speech to a group of heads, but fail to make eye contact with a single person. In other words, you're looking at everybody (hose-piping), but not really looking at anybody.

Eye contact is a powerful visual cue that lets your audience know you are addressing them personally. Though it may not be possible to make eye contact with everyone (especially in a large conference-style speech), by making a direct visual connection with a small percentage of the group, you convey the impression of personal attention to everyone in your audience.

Making eye contact is not about staring down a selected group of participants. It's about delivering one particular point to one particular individual at a time. The following exercise will help you to master this important skill.

Exercise

Set up four empty chairs in a room. Space them out so that they cover each of the four major quadrants of a room, and place one magazine, open to a face in a full-page ad, on each seat.

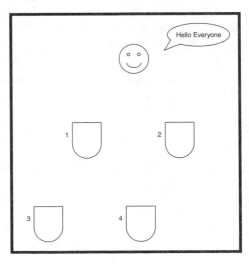

Start delivering your talk and first focus on the face in chair number 1. Speak to that person as if there was nobody else in the room. (That's right: There isn't.) Keep doing this until you are satisfied that you have gotten your point across to this imaginary individual.

Continue with your speech, but now focus on chair number 2. Deliver this part of your presentation to that person. Once again, keep doing this until you feel you have successfully brought your point home. Repeat this process with chair numbers 3 and 4.

Now it's time to bring it all together. Deliver your speech from the beginning, randomly making eye contact with the faces on different chairs to make your point. For example: Start with chair number 3, then deliver the next part to chair number 1, then chair number 2, and so on. Do this until you feel that you are communicating to individual chairs (people) rather than an anonymous group.

You can use this same pattern of eye contact when speaking in front of a live audience. Simply make eye contact with random individuals in different parts of the room. Spend five or 10 seconds delivering your point to each person and then move on to the next. In a large audience where it's impossible to focus on individuals towards the back, make eye contact with small groups. By focusing on individuals, rather than hose-piping, you will end up speaking *to* your audience, rather than *at* them.

Enunciate and Articulate

Elocution, articulation, diction, and enunciation—they all add up to the same thing: Pronounce your words clearly and distinctly! One of the most exhausting experiences for an audience is listening to a speaker who slurs his/her words together, drops syllables, and in general plays fast and loose with the enunciation of the English language. The most common articulation crimes include:

Dropping G's

Thinking become *think-in*
Selling become *sell-in*
Walking become *walk-in*
Jogging becomes *jog-in*
Talking become *talk-in*

Smashing Words Together

Will you becomes *will-ya*
Ought to becomes *ot-ta*
Have to become *haf-ta*
Want to becomes *wan-na*
What I becomes *Wa-di*

To test your own skill, take the following enunciation exam. Tape record yourself saying the following sentences out loud, naturally, without thinking them through.

I'm going to have to think about that one. Do you know what I mean?

I ought to tell my bank that I will be selling the car and paying them back for the loan.

I don't know why you want to go jogging that early in the morning.

How did you do? Did you drop any G's? Contract any words? Here is what these sound like when not enunciated properly:

I'm gon-na haf-ta think bout that one. Do ya know wa-di mean?

I ot-ta tell my bank that I will be sell-in the car and pay-in um back fur the loan.

I dun-no why you wan-na go jog-in that early in the mornin.

Exercise

The best way to improve your ability to articulate is to practice, practice, and practice. Diction exercises will help you get into the habit of speaking clearly.

Your best bet is to stand in front of a mirror, so you can watch how your tongue, lips, and face move when you are enunciating accurately. Here are a few to try out.

1. Sally sells seashells down by the seashore for a small but sizable sum.

2. Three green grasshoppers were in the grass grazing and guzzling.

3. Presenters who proffer profound, personal patter are popular.

4. Around and round, the rough and ragged room, the rugged reporter ran.

Use Sensory Language

If you listen closely, most speakers will tend to favor words that relate to one of the following senses:

Visual: "That's clear to me."

Auditory: "I hear what you are saying."

Tactile: "I feel your pain."

Using sensory language (a combination of visual, auditory, and tactile words) creates rapport with your audience *and* helps hold their interest. Neutral language, on the other hand, may contain all the facts, but often leaves listeners cold. Consider how the following examples come across:

"I come from a dusty town 30 miles south of nowhere in Kentucky. It seems like I spent the first 10 years of my life watching lazy cows slowly move across gentle hillsides. I remember sitting on warm grass, drinking lemonade, and listening to the excited twitter of Purple Martins as they prepared for their long journey south."

Compared to:

"I am from a small town in southern Kentucky. My parents were farmers, so I spent the first few years of my childhood on the land."

The first example utilizes the power of sensory language by forming an experience the audience can easily relate to. The richness of the words (*watching, slowly, gentle, warm, listening, twitter*) appeals to the listeners' senses rather than their intellect. By speaking this way, the presenter triggers a gut reaction that quickly grabs the audience's attention.

The second example uses neutral language that focuses mainly on the facts. Speaking this way will appeal to an audience's intellect, but won't connect with them emotionally, because it's colder and less colorful.

Public Speaking In An Instant

Learning to integrate all three modes of sensory language into your presentation is a critical because since different audience members will have different sensory preferences. Therefore, to reach everyone, be sure to use words and phrases that cover all the senses.

Sense	Words	Phrases
Visual words and phrases paint pictures and conjure up images.	Clear Focus Clarify Vision Perspective Observe See/View	*"It looks good to me!"* *"What is your view on the matter?"* *"My recollection is cloudy."* *"I would like you to shed some light on a few things."* *"We went through a whole spectrum of ideas."* *"The purpose seems a little hazy."* *"Suddenly it dawned on me...."* *"Life is not always black and white."*
Auditory words and phrases add tone to what is being said.	Hear Tell Sound Volume Tone Say Listen	*"Let me explain."* *"Your name rings a bell."* *"The ground rules had to be drummed into them."* *"My idea brought about peals of laughter."* *"The team had a lot of harmony."* *"Suddenly the idea just clicked."* *"The delivery update was music to my ears."*
Tactile words and phrases spell out physical conditions and emotional feelings.	Touch Firm Feel Pressure Rough Solid Smooth	*"It just feels right."* *"Warm regards."* *"It didn't take much to get her inflamed."* *"Hold on; this could be a bumpy ride!"* *"The manager has a hands-on approach."* *"She's so light on her feet."* *"I can't do it now. I'm too pressed for time."* *"Their reception to the idea was cool at first."*

	Bland Fragrant Swallow Sick Sweet Tasty Tart	"He said that my idea _stinks._" "I thought the presentation was too _vanilla._" "Before I make a decision I need time to _digest_ all the facts." "The new organizational changes are _sugar coating._" "It was in poor _taste._" "This idea _reeks_ of manipulation." "He has a _sweet_ disposition!" "I _smell_ success!"
Taste and **Smell** words and phrases add strong sentiment.		

Exercise

Consider several points you want to make in an upcoming speech and write a sentence conveying that point in the given sensory mode written here:

Point #1:

_____

Said in a visual way:

_____

Point #2:

_____

Said in an auditory way:

_____

Point #3:

_____

Said in a tactile way:

_____

Watch Out for Word Blunders

The English language seems full of words and phrases that are designed to be mispronounced. Even the word *pronunciation* (pro-NUN-see-A-shun) gets all muddled up and comes out as the incorrect pro-NOUN-see-A-shun. Though it may seem like nitpicking, good speakers say their words as meant to be spoken. What words or phrases do you tend to tangle? Following are some of the most commonly mangled utterances and their correct articulation.

Word	Do Say:	Please Don't Say:
Affidavit	Af-fi-da-VIT	Af-fi-da-VID
Arctic	ARC-tic	AR-tic
Asterisk	as-ter-ISK	as-ter-IK
Athlete	ATH-leet	ath-A-leet
Candidate	kan-DI-dayt	kan-I-dayt
Disastrous	di-zas-TRES	di-zas-TER-es
Et cetera	ET-set-er-a	EK-set-er-a
Espresso	ESS-press-oh	EX-press-oh
February	Feb-ROO-air-y	Feb-YOO-air-y
Minuscule	min-UH-skyool	min-IH-skyool
Mischievous	mis-CHE-vus	mis-CHEE-vee-us
Nuclear	noo-KLEE-ur	noo-KYU-lur
Percolate	perc-O-late	perc-U-late
Prescription	PRIH-skrip-shun	PER-skrip-shun
Realtor	REAL-tor	real-A-tor
Ticklish	tik-LISH	tik-A-lish
Triathlon	try-ATH-lon	try-ath-A-lon
Utmost	UT-most	UP-most

If you found any words you mispronounce in this list (don't feel bad—most of us have) practice saying and writing the correct way several times. Once your brain has established a new neural pathway to the proper pronunciation, you are well on your way to better English.

Trivial Pursuits

Talking in a hurry can lead to a habit of *haplology*—the dropping of one of two identical syllables such as the [ob] and [ab] in the word *probably*. Mispronounced it becomes prob-LY.

Phrases That Get All Fouled Up

A cardSHARP will take your money at the poker table. But call it the incorrect card SHARK and a lingering linguist will eat you alive.

The saying it's a dog-EAT-dog world, may sound less kind than a doggy-dog world, but the first phrase is the correct one.

It's bad business to take thing for GRANTED, but even worse to say you are taking them for GRANITE.

And just for good measure, there is no such word as IRREGARDLESS. The word is REGARDLESS, regardless of what you might have thought!

Video Tape Your Presentations

Many speakers ask for their speeches to be video taped and will often pay to have this done. Here are a few good reasons why you may want to voluntarily step into the light:

Self-Improvement

There is nothing as enlightening (and occasionally horrifying) as seeing yourself on video. It provides a great opportunity to step back and objectively assess your strengths and weaknesses as a speaker.

Capture Good Material

Not every speech you give, on the same topic, will be exactly the same, every time. Chances are you will say something that is brilliant—spontaneously! Video lets you capture these magic moments for all eternity.

Analyze Audience Response

Reviewing your videotape will help you to identify where in the speech you were connecting with your audience, what material they responded the strongest to, and what parts they found funny.

Create Products

If you're a consultant, trainer, author, or professional speaker, you can increase the amount of money you make from each engagement by offering video and or audiotapes of your presentations for sale.

Promotion and Marketing

Almost everyone will ask you for your demo tape before they hire you to give a presentation. Having an up-to-date, spiffy reel that demonstrates your brilliance and panache is an audition for your next speaking gig.

Be Video-Friendly

At convention speeches, all-hands meetings, and large conferences, it's common practice to video tape the speaker and show a live feed of his/her presentation on giant screens to the left and right of the stage. This allows audience members in the back of the room to clearly see and hear what the speaker is doing and saying. Video-enhanced meetings present specific logistical situations you should be aware of.

For example: The use of video also means the use of lights—big, bright lights that will be pointing directly at you. If you're the type of speaker who likes to make face-to-face contact with your audience, the blinding blackness caused by large lights shining in your face can come as a shock. Many inexperienced speakers try to look out, beyond the illumination, to the audience. They end up squinting, shading their eyes, and hesitantly trying to peer into the murk. As you might imagine, this mole-like behavior is unattractive and sets completely the wrong tone for your talk. You can better prepare for this situation by rehearsing your presentation while staring at a blank wall so that you learn to deliver your discourse, without depending on visual feedback.

Speaker Savvy: *Limit your movements to the central area of the platform and resist the urge to wander into dimly lit areas.*

In addition to working with lights, be sure to check the camera angles on your speech before you begin. Once the cameras are set up and in place, have an assistant stand in the general area where you will be speaking. Take a peek through the camera lens and make sure that any pillars, lecterns, and so forth won't obscure you. Also, can your audiovisuals be seen from this angle?

Lastly, don't play to the camera. The best strategy (if you can manage it) is to forget that the camera exists and focus on the audience—even if you can't see them.

Practice Small-Group Savvy

When planning for a public speaking engagement, it's important to consider the size of your audience, as the listening style of a smaller group is distinct from that of a large one. When presenting to an audience of fewer than 15 people, keep the following three things in mind to ensure that your presentation to a small group makes a big impact:

Sit instead of stand. Whereas it's standard practice for a speaker to stand in front of the group when making a presentation, if you only have a handful of people in the audience, it makes more sense to sit down. Doing this helps close the gap between you and your listeners because it puts you all, literally, on the same level.

Encourage questions throughout. It's normal when presenting in front of large audiences to leave time at the end for a Q&A session. With a small group, you can create more participation and encourage dialogue by allowing people to ask questions and share their insights as you go along. Let the group know upfront that instead of a Q&A period at the end, you encourage them to share their comments and queries as they arise.

Use an informal room setup. The following diagram shows a typical, classroom-style seating arrangement applied to a small group setting.

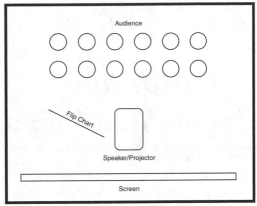

Formal Room Setup for Small Groups

Although this is an effective arrangement for larger groups, notice how formal, even intimidating, it can seem for a smaller one. If you plan on using overhead slides, a semi-circular, or horseshoe shape (see the following diagram) is a good choice because it will allow all the participants to see each other and the visual aids at the same time. If you don't plan on using visuals, a circular setup, such as sitting around a rectangular or oval conference table, works well.

Speaker Savvy: *If you are using a flip chart, position it at an angle, off to the side, so that everyone (including you) can see it.*

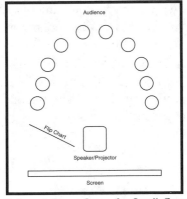

Informal Room Setup for Small Groups

Manage Medium-Sized Groups

Most of the presentations you will give in a businesses setting (such as meetings, sales pitches, marketing overviews, and so on) will be medium-sized and involve an average of 20–40 attendees. One advantage of a group this size is that you can see everyone in the room. But unlike smaller gatherings, which by design are more intimate, medium-sized groups require a few additional speaker strategies for connecting with your audience.

Speak louder than normal. It's natural to think that, if you speak in your normal tone of voice, everyone in the room (including those in the back row) will be able to hear you. But few presenters realize the actual volume needed to capture and sustain the attention of 40 people. Hint: It's louder than you think. One surefire way to set your volume is to deliver a few lines of your presentation (in the designated room) to an assistant at the back and adjust accordingly based on his/her feedback. Remember that when the room is filled, some of the sound will be absorbed, so you will have to speak even louder than at the run-through!

Plan a center aisle. The seating arrangements for this size group will almost always be classroom-style. Before your presentation, confirm the seating setup shown in the following diagram and make sure a center aisle is included.

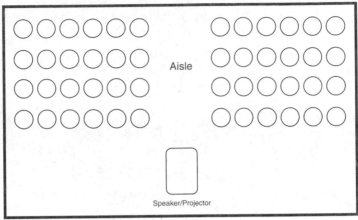

Room Setup for Medium-Sized Groups

Speaker Savvy: *If you want to get up close and personal with the group, walk up and down the center aisle. Clinging to the podium, though offering a bit of security, can make your talk static and lifeless. Live dangerously and roam about the room so that everyone feels as if you are talking to them.*

Use audience member's names. The sooner you get people participating, the sooner you build rapport and put everyone at ease. Instead of giving neutral and anonymous examples, such as *"With our new system, an employee can quickly pull up all the information they need to answer a customer's ordering question,"* include actual names of the people in the group. For example: *"Let's say that Jane is a customer who calls in with an ordering question; if Ramone is the person taking that call, all he has to do is punch in the customer number and all the information is instantly displayed."* Doing this a few times at the beginning of your presentation lets people know that you know who they are—and they will respond accordingly.

Define a period for questions. In a group this size, you have the option of allowing the participants to ask questions as you go along or waiting until the end and conducting a Q&A session. If you allow spontaneous questions throughout, you will occasionally have to graciously handle a question that takes too long to answer or would shift you too far off track. In either case, remember to paraphrase and repeat back the question asked for the group's benefit.

Connect With Large Groups

One of the challenges of speaking to large audiences (250 people or more) is striking a balance between giving a well-organized, information-driven presentation and creating affinity and rapport with the group. With meetings of this size, speakers can seem distant and isolated as they peer out from behind the podium. To gain and maintain the group's full attention, try the following:

Stand on a platform. To be clearly seen (and to see) any group of more than 100 participants, stand on a platform or riser. For an audience of a few hundred people, an 8- or 12-inch riser is adequate, but if you are presenting for a few thousand (say at a convention) you'll need even more height.

Speaker Savvy: Request that even a large room be set up according to the following diagram. Having an aisle in the middle of the room breaks up the solid block of people that can suppress audience participation.

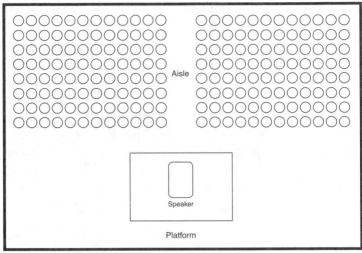

Room Setup for Large Groups

Use a wireless lavaliere microphone. Whenever possible, avoid getting stuck behind a static microphone that is attached to a podium or a handheld microphone that you need to hold throughout your entire speech. Instead, request a wireless lavaliere. This is a tiny microphone that attaches to your tie or dress, connected to a small battery-powered transmitter that clips to your belt. It allows complete freedom of movement and lets you walk away from the podium and make full use of the space at the front of the room. If you are adventurous, you can even step down into the group for a minute if there are stairs conveniently situated at the front of the platform.

Exaggerate your gestures and voice. Formal presentations, which run on a pre-planned time line and an organized script, work the best with large groups. But to minimize the "distant and isolated" feeling that can accompany this type of presentation, you want to use exaggerated body language and tone of voice to bring excitement and interest to what you are saying. For example: Really big arm movements (that may seem wildly exaggerated to you) fill up the space and can add animation to your presentation. Likewise, normal speech patterns can sound monotone in a big group, so you'll grab more attention by punching up your inflection. In other words, this is one case in which you want to let the little disc jockey inside of you run free.

Get answers by raised hands. Include the audience from the beginning of your talk by asking them questions that they respond to by raising their hands. For example: If you were giving a talk on workplace safety, you might ask, "How many of you have had a workman's comp claim in the past six months? Please raise your hands." This works best if you model the body language by raising your hand as you ask the question. This technique is an efficient—and silent—way for your audience to be actively engaged in the conversation.

Set up a microphone for questions. To ensure that everyone in the group can hear the questions asked, have a wireless, handheld microphone station available for the Q&A session. If the audience is very large or spread out, set up several microphone stations throughout the room.

Ask rhetorical questions. Because large groups don't allow you the freedom to ask direct questions and have them be answered by the group, use rhetorical questions instead. For example: If your presentation is about the advantages of a newly installed, company-wide computer system, ask a question that you know everyone will unanimously agree to such as, "How many of you had problems with invoicing on the old system?" Or, "How many of you wanted to throw the computer out the window on those days when it was slower than molasses?"

Be Funny

Humor is no laughing matter, especially for those speakers for whom being funny does not come naturally. If you think of yourself as humor-challenged, consider it a worthwhile goal to go beyond your "serious" zone and make your audience laugh. Using humor helps your audience disregard any differences of style and viewpoint you may have. Mark Twain was spot on when he noted, "Against the assault of laughter, nothing can stand." If you're up for the challenge of making your speech more laughable (in the best sense of the word), try out the following do's and don'ts.

Don't tell a joke.

Regardless of how funny your family thinks you are, you are not a stand-up comedian. Jay Leno and Jerry Seinfeld are, so leave the timing and clever stuff to them.

Don't use humor that doesn't fit.

Telling a funny story that has nothing to do with your presentation topic will make your humor humorless. People have an implicit expectation that the things you talk about will relate to your topic and, when they don't, the group's goodwill can become strained.

Don't announce what's funny.

Humor is best when it is woven into the fabric of your story, not announced up front. For example: Prefacing a funny story by saying, "I've got a really funny story to tell you," separates it from the natural flow of the narrative and removes the element of delightful surprise.

Don't make fun of those in less-powerful positions.

All humor to some degree is based on making fun of some person, situation, or event. But joking about those with no power will come across as mean, not funny.

Do draw upon your personal experience.

A few years ago comedian Rick Reynolds wrote and performed a one-man show called "Only the Truth Is Funny." This is good advice for a speaker. Rather than concoct elaborate accounts designed to have your audience rolling in the aisles—think local, simple, and real. What has happened to you or your friends that demonstrates your point? Look for the humor in everyday events and your audience will find it funny because they will be better able to relate to the situation.

Do keep your stories short.

If you've ever been on the receiving end of a long, drawn-out joke or story you know that, at some point, you are just waiting for it to end. The longer a story drags on, the less any punch line can live up to the long winding road that preceded it.

Do use humor that you think is funny.

Everyone has a different idea of what is funny. So even if your story isn't funny to everyone, the spirit in which you communicate it can be infectious. If you find the anecdote funny, then your pleasure in telling it will be appreciated and enjoyed by all.

Do use humor that is appropriate to your audience.

Are your listeners formal or informal, artistic or technical, male or female, conservative or liberal? Allow the composition of your audience to guide the type of humor you use. Be sure to remove any material that might offend, upset, or alienate you from the group and leverage any opportunity to give people a chance to laugh at themselves. For example: The humor you might use with a group of stevedores would no doubt be distinctly different from that you would use with a group of seamstresses.

Observe the Rules of Comedy

Although nobody, including professional comedians, tells old-fashioned, *"take my wife please"* type of jokes any more, they still use time-tested techniques to make people laugh. Borrowing a page from the book of modern stand-up comedy, almost anyone can use the following simple techniques to make their presentation just a bit funnier, or at least a little livelier.

Look for commonality. There are certain situations, contexts, and emotions (for example: the frustration of trying to correct an error on a credit report) that are universal to everyone in the room. Making fun of experiences that your audience shares is entertaining, but joking about obscure things, that only you can relate to, is not.

Go local. No matter how funny you think your joke is, if your audience can't relate to it, they won't laugh. One way to get giggles is to customize your content to the local places and customs of your audience.

Be current. Comedy is about the now, not yesterday. Saying *"20 years ago, when I was walking down the street"* does not pack the same punch as putting things it in the present by saying *"earlier, when I was taking my morning walk."*

Follow up funny. Sometimes called callbacks or tags, the concept is if they laughed at it once, they will again. If you hit upon a punch line (a funny idea, word, or phrase) in your speech that makes your audience laugh, bring it back later in the speech for a repeat performance. The same humorous statement the second and sometimes third time around can be effective. In other words, work your funny stuff. Be warned, however, that more than three repeats and your joke goes from funny to flat.

Be specific. The better picture you paint and the more details you include, the funnier the situation you are describing will be. For example: Your office is not *messy* (general) but rather was declared *condemned due to Chinese takeout container overload by the human resources department* (specific).

Act out. If you can pull it off, don't be afraid to imitate (not mock) the voice or body language of someone in the story you are telling. Hand gestures, facial expressions, posture, and vocal variety can add humor and spice.

Exaggerate. Taking things to the extreme one way or another, is often an entry point for entertainment. For example: *"The dress code at our office has become so relaxed that I came to work in my pajamas yesterday and no one noticed!"*

Go K. Seriously, for some reason, Americans find words beginning with a K sound funnier than other words (who knew?). So instead of *"eating donuts, at the morning sales meeting"*] try *"chowing down on Krispy Kremes at the company off site."*

Make up a mondegreen. A mondegreen is a lyric of a song or other phrase that is misheard and misspoken. For example: People often think the phrase *it's a dog-eat-dog world* is the incorrect *it's a doggy dog world.*

Entertain Your Audience

Entertaining speeches are just that. Their primary purpose is to have your audience sit back, relax, and enjoy themselves—hopefully with a good sense of humor along the way. Humor, which can be hard to define—and even harder to deliver—is a key ingredient in amusing an audience. To prepare for an entertaining presentation, think about what kinds of situations your group are likely to find themselves in. What are their interests? What inside jokes and jargon do they use? Once you have an idea of their unique circumstances, the following techniques will help you tickle their funny bone.

Understatement

This is the art of deliberately playing down an important issue or fact. For example: *"The airline told us that there was going to be a short delay in boarding because the plane had a technical problem. Great, I thought, this will give me time to get something to eat. Forty-eight hours later I had tried every restaurant in the airport."*

Unexpected Twists and Turns

Audiences like to be surprised, so an out-of-the-blue ending will leave them amused. For example: *"My mother called a bookstore on the phone the other day to see if they had a book she was looking for in stock. The clerk who answered the phone politely told her, 'I'm sorry I can't tell you that right now; the computer's down.' Thinking that was the end of the story the clerk thanked my mother for calling and was about to hang up. 'Wait a minute' my mom jumped in. 'Why don't you just go physically look on the shelf and see if it's there?' she inquired. 'Wow,' said the clerk in amazement. 'I hadn't thought of that.'"*

Irony

Irony is that absurd and funny disparity between what you say and what your audience expects you to say. Saying the opposite of what is logical, can catch your audience off guard—in a good way. For example: *"We have several clients overseas, and recently I went to London to visit one of them. I was delighted to find that there is no longer any smoking allowed in the pubs. Unfortunately, everyone now drinks in the streets so they can smoke. On this trip I had more trouble finding fresh air outside than inside!"*

Puns

These are words that have two meanings. For example: *"My original company manufactured bed comforters and pillows. We used man-made fibers for the filling, as well as goose-feathers. We made a greater profit on the polyester products—because the cost of **down** went **up**."*

Used sparingly, puns can be entertaining and clever—but be warned: Overused, they are tiresome.

Motivate Your Audience

Motivational speeches are by nature designed to encourage and inspire an audience to action. The goal of your presentation may be to reinforce a company initiative, get staff excited about a new product promotion, or sell your services to a potential client. Regardless, the following ideas will help pump up your powers of persuasion:

Establish Common Ground

Let your audience know the ways in which you can personally relate to their specific needs and circumstances. People are more receptive to what you are offering if they feel you feel their pain. For example: *"My business has changed a great deal over the past year. One significant difference is the skyrocketing cost of fuel. I, like you, am continually looking for ways to reduce my transportation costs. This has been increasingly difficult and is a constant challenge."*

Another way of creating rapport and closing the gap between yourself and the audience is to communicate the shared common beliefs you both hold about your topic. For example: *"Many industry insiders believe that the cost of fuel will just keep going up, and most of us*

are looking for alternative, cleaner energy sources to replace the tradi-
tional ones—but feel that the current options are very limited."

Let Your Audience Know
What to Expect

Let your audience know exactly what you are speaking about,
why it's important, and what you guess their response will be. For
example, making a presentation to a prospective client, you might
say: *"Thank you for inviting us here today to present our five-step solution
to your training needs. We are specialists in multimedia training and we
believe that what we have come up with will not only meet your requirements—
but also offer an implementation process that you will find easy, efficient,
and cost-effective."*

This technique creates an expectation of how your audience
will react. Consequently, you must be fairly certain that you can
deliver on your word! If you suspect that you will be presenting to a
skeptical audience, use the same technique, but soften the message a bit. The changes to the first message are marked in bold:
*"Thank you for inviting us here today to present our five-step solution to
your training needs. We are specialists in multimedia training and we
hope that what we have come up with will not only meet your requirements—
but also offer an implementation process that **will make your life easier.**"*

Tell a Story That Inspires

Well-told stories work because they have a universal appeal that
audiences are able to personally relate to. Using examples of people
who have defied the odds, or accomplished the impossible, inspires
in others the confidence to step out of their comfort zone and try
something new. For example: *"I have never been much for exercise. In
fact, my gym membership card rarely saw the light of day. Then, a while
ago, I was visiting Yosemite and I looked up at El Capitan and there in
the distance I saw two colored specks—climbers making their way to the
top. I was about to make a remark about how climbers are a certain*

breed with stronger, muscular bodies, etc., when my wife said she had heard on the radio that one of the climbers was paralyzed from the waist down. This was to be the first ever successful ascent of El Capitan by a paraplegic. I was humbled and realized that all my excuses for not exercising were insignificant compared with what I had just witnessed."

Use Emotional Color

When describing an experience, use descriptive words and phrases to portray what was happening and being felt. For example: *"The bull wasn't interested in me when I first walked through the pasture. Then it turned and looked right into my eyes. Immediately, my knees went rubbery. I felt the burning desire to run—but where? I was paralyzed with fear...."*

Address Opposing Viewpoints Head-On

Motivation does not mean ignoring the concerns, questions, and various viewpoints held by your audience members. On the contrary, it means embracing and addressing them as well as offering up alternative ways of viewing the situation. For example:

"When I talk about giving cash bonuses to your best-performing staff, I know some of you are thinking but...."

"We can't afford that!"

"They'll just keep expecting more every year."

"Why give them a bonus for what they're paid to do in the first place?"

"I can certainly understand why you feel this way, but I want to ask you to look at this from a fresh perspective for a moment. Let's consider some recent studies...."

Educate Your Audience

Different presentations have different purposes, so the way you design and deliver your speech will vary accordingly. If the primary purpose of your presentation is to inform your audience (about procedures, techniques, research, product information, and so on), the following guidelines will help maximize your impact:

- **Avoid information overload and only present one point at a time.** Don't rush; your audience needs time to digest the information you are presenting.

- **Use your introduction to preview your key points.** This creates a framework for what you are going to talk about and provides the audience with a road map of what's to come.

- **Graphically present your key points.** They say that a picture is worth a thousand words, so using a program such as PowerPoint to display graphs, tables, diagrams, and headlines will make your ideas more easily understood.

- **Provide handouts.** Handouts should contain the highlights of your speech but not all the details. Too much information is a temptation, and you can lose your audience's attention if they are busy reading ahead.

- **Use analogies.** An analogy is a comparison between two things that are similar in some respects. Analogies are a great tool to help you explain something or make it easier to understand. For example: If you were speaking about the advantages of broadband technology—over old-fashioned dial-up—you might compare the amount of water that flows through a drainpipe with the limited flow of water going through a drinking straw.

- **Provide the who, what, when, and where.** Describe important points in your speech by giving your audience information about who was involved, what they were doing or saying, and when and where the event took place.

- **Make full use of your senses.** Provide your audience with sensory information such as this: How did the scene look? What were the sounds you heard? Was there a smell or a taste that stands out?

- **Explain why your information is useful.** With the pressures of today's workplace, people don't want to waste their time, even with a nice speaker like you. Consequently, your audience will pay more attention if you explain how your topic translates into a benefit for them.

- **Clarify the problem your information will help solve.** Your audience (like everyone) is looking for simple and fast (dare we say *In An Instant*) solutions to their problems. By relating your topic to real-world issues that affect your audience, you engage their interest and make your talk timely.

Give a Great Toast

On various occasions throughout your work life you will be asked to give a toast. Perhaps you will have the honor of speaking at a colleague's retirement dinner, or welcoming a new vice president at the annual company meeting, or presenting an award to the winning team of this month's sales competition. Whatever the occasion, if you have been tasked with the job of toasting, consider yourself lucky, not cursed!

For most people, the truly terrifying part of toasting is not standing up and talking, but figuring out what they are going to say in the first place. The best strategy is to pre-write your toast and practice it before the actual event, keeping in mind the following general guidelines:

- Limit your toast to one or two minutes—especially if other people are also going to speak.
- Mention your relationship (client, colleague, cousin) with the toastee.
- Say the honored guest's name both at the beginning and at the end of the toast.
- Weave in a short personal memory, story, or comment about the person.
- Do some basic research on the audience. What will they find moving or humorous?
- Avoid any comments that might be hurtful or embarrassing.
- Don't read verbatim from your notes. Instead, memorize what you want to say and use the notes as a cue sheet.

Secure in what you are going to say, your first job on the day of the event is to address some basic logistics. *Are you standing in a spot where you can be seen by everyone in the room? Is the honoree currently in the room? Does everyone have access to water/wine/champagne to fill their glass?*

Speaker Savvy: *Before your toast, go out of your way to connect with a few people in the audience. When you speak, you can focus on these folks to start.*

Logistics having been settled, confidently clink your glass to garner the group's attention. Take a deep breath and a moment or two to connect with the audience, and begin. With a little planning you can deliver a tribute that will be remembered long after the occasion has passed. A few on-the-spot strategies to keep in mind include:

- Make the first and last person you look at the person you are toasting.
- Connect with the entire audience by scanning the room and looking at them during the toast.
- Either keep your glass on the table until you are ready to pick it up, or hold it in front of your chest.
- Avoid gesturing with your glass. This prevents spillage (and embarrassment).
- When ready, raise your glass to eye level and speak directly at the person you are toasting.
- Take a sip, not a slug, of your drink.

Exercise

Think of a person you are planning on toasting at an upcoming event. Answer the following questions in the space provided.

What are one or two authentic compliments I want to give this person?

_____

What is a simple story or example that illustrates some quality I want to appreciate this person for?

_____

What does this person mean to me?

_____

What does this person means to others?

_____

Deliver an Eloquent Eulogy

In the face of grief, many people find it challenging to stand up and speak about a colleague or friend who has recently passed away. Yet, the act of describing the richness of another person's life, and all the emotion that goes with it, can serve to help the healing process; celebrate and honor the other person's life; express sincere gratitude for his/her contribution; and bring closure and affirm what can be learned. No one is ever *prepared* to deliver a eulogy, but taking the time to plan will help you speak authentically and eloquently about the lost loved one.

Select the memories you want to share. As you reflect on the stories and situations from the person's life, note the important points that each scene illustrates. For example:

- What did you admire about the person?
- What qualities did they posses?
- What accomplishments did they achieve?
- What will you miss most about them?
- What will you remember most about them?

These moments do not have to be extraordinary; sometimes a seemingly insignificant memory contains the essence of that person and your relationship with him/her. Remember that your mission is to bring the person's spirit into the minds of those assembled and paint a picture of who he/she was. Once you have taken the time to look back, choose a few reminiscences and their meaning, and write them down.

Speaker Savvy: Consider finishing with a short poem that expresses your feelings about the other person.

Invite contributions from other people. You can offer a great gift to those mourners who can't attend the service by asking them to contribute stories and remembrances of the deceased. By incorporating their memories and words into your eulogy, you deepen understanding of the departed's life while honoring those who cannot attend.

Prepare notes. Because eulogies are often so deeply felt, it's better to deliver them in a prepared but spontaneous way, rather than reading them like a speech. To do this, use a 5-inch-by-7-inch index card and write a few words on each line for each point you want to make. Use large capital letters written with a black marking pen so that you can easily see what's written by quickly glancing down at the card, rather than having to squint and strain.

Accept the waves of emotion. When overtaken with grief, it can be difficult to speak. If this happens, don't try to "tough your way through it." Instead, stop speaking and give your emotions room to breathe (keep a handkerchief or tissues handy). When you're ready, continue on, knowing that your display of feelings—while often considered taboo in public—is natural and an important part of your, and the other mourners', healing process.

Follow a few guidelines. Although there is no "right" way to deliver a eulogy, there are a few guidelines you should follow.

- The eulogy should be about five minutes in length. If you are not sure about the timing, use your prepared outline to practice and track what you are going to say. If you come out at longer than seven minutes, edit it down by removing a story or two.

- Let the mourners know who you are and your relationship to the deceased.

- Stay positive, and use loving humor when describing the person's personal quirks and eccentricities. A eulogy is not the time to air your unfinished business.

For specific ideas and examples of eulogies, see Garry Schaeffer's book, *A Labor of Love: How to Write a Eulogy* (GMS Publications, 2006).

Participate on a Panel

At some point in your career you *will* be asked to speak on a panel. One challenge is that you can't control this type of presentation in the same way you can when you're flying solo. If you decide to say "yes" to a panel discussion, here are a few rules of the game to ensure your success.

Don't just educate your audience; entertain them. Being a panelist is more than simply imparting accurate information and providing pithy answers to the moderator's questions—it's also about being interesting to listen to. Most panelists are so concerned with getting their point across they forget to infuse their speaking with humor and energy.

Keep your answers short and snappy. Because the moderator may ask every panelist to answer the same question from his/her point of view, it's important to keep your responses simple and on target. Know ahead of time the key points you want to make, and practice getting them across in a concise way.

Don't rely on the moderator to come up with an introduction for you personally. Remember that he/she has three to 10 people to introduce. Instead, write a short bio that introduces you and send it to the moderator before the event. Just to be on the safe side, also have a copy on hand to give him/her at the event itself.

Speaker Savvy: Be sure the moderator knows exactly how to pronounce both your name and your company's name.

Pay attention when other panelists speak. When you are not talking, your attention should be respectfully focused on whoever is. Looking bored, reading through your notes, polishing your fingernails, or other non-attentive behavior, is disrespectful to your colleagues and makes you look like an amateur.

Don't compete with the other panelists. Everyone on the panel is there to provide their own unique perspective and expertise. There's no need for you to address what the other panelists have said by agreeing or disagreeing with their comments. Instead, focus on the message you want to deliver.

Be available to talk after the panel. Because of the limited time each panelist has to get his/her message across, there may be audience members who want to speak with you in person after the event. Don't rush off after the presentation, but instead plan on hanging around for a bit to give the participants, and perhaps even potential clients, the chance to pick your brain.

A Few Words on Being the Panel Moderator

Moderating a panel can be even more challenging than speaking on one. Your job requires you to be on stage the whole time, but not the center of attention. Here are three tips on how to be a pro at panel moderation:

- Don't talk to much. You are not a panelist, but the facilitator of the discussion. Ask questions as appropriate, but don't interject your side comments or asides.

- Know your stuff. This means prepare ahead of time by knowing who the panelists are, what their areas of expertise are, and what questions you plan on asking them.

- Keep strict control of the time. Have a system devised upfront to let panelists know if they are going over their allotted time to answer a question. It's your job to make sure the panel begins and ends on time and that all panelists get a fair shake at answering questions and making their points.

Make the Best of Banquet Speaking

If you have been invited to speak at a function where people will be seated at tables eating a meal (and perhaps drinking some wine), you have a special challenge ahead of you. Banquet speaking can get the goat of the best of speakers, so pay attention to the following details to ensure that your message makes it past the participant's clanking china and clattering silverware:

Avoid too many details. Despite our multitasking mentality, most people can't eat, talk, and listen to a great deal of detail—all at the same time. Make it easier for everyone by keeping your topic fairly general, rather than overly specific. For example: Getting seriously bogged down in the details of how to balance this year's budget using the new Money Manager 2.0 will be no competition for the chocolate lava cake being served up for dessert!

Learn to talk to the backs of heads. People at banquets are most often seated at large round tables, so it is inevitable that some of the group will have their backs to you. Gradually, as you grab their attention with your pearls of wisdom and thrill them with your clever banter, many will turn around to face you—but not necessarily all. Don't take this as a personal insult. Instead, learn to deliver your talk with the same amount of confidence and enthusiasm as you would if they were looking at you.

Place the tables close together. Banquet speaking is hard enough without a room setup that emphasizes distance. In advance of your presentation, talk with the meeting planner or room setup supervisor and request that they place the tables as close together as possible, allowing enough room for the wait staff to maneuver. Often by default, the hotel or banquet facility will spread the tables out as far as possible to fill the room. This has the impact of making the space feel even larger and can put a damper on participation.

Speaker Savvy: If possible, ask that the speaker area not be set up in front of or directly next to the doors where wait staff will be going in and out to service the meal.

Include the noise. The clanking of silverware, the dropping of dishes, the banging of doors as waiters walk in and out—all par for the course with banquet speaking. If you show irritation or aggravation every time a clink, clank, or clunk occurs, your reactions will become more distracting than the noise itself. Expect it to be noisy, speak louder, and deal with it.

Speaker Savvy: Organize the service so that all bussing of tables stops for the first 10 minutes of your talk, because this is a critical time for you to engage the audience.

Give a five-minute warning. Let the group know when they have five minutes left to lift off. This allows them to grab a quick cup of coffee, go through the buffet line for one more biscuit, or make a quick call and be back in their seats, ready to start when you are.

Do a Good Job Breaking Bad News

At some point in your work life you will probably be called upon to make a presentation where you are the bearer of bad news. Perhaps you'll have to announce a pending company merger that threatens layoffs, a reorganization requiring staff relocation, or poor sales results that demand some uncomfortable belt-tightening. Regardless, the skills required vary a bit from regular presentations. If you have the unenviable job of breaking bad news, follow these guidelines to make it as painless as possible—for you and them:

Don't act guilty or hesitant. You are more than likely *not* the cause of the unpleasant circumstances, but rather the messenger. Your job is to show confidence and compassion rather than timidity and tentativeness. Focusing on concerns such as "they won't like me," "they'll think of me as a hatchet-man," or "they'll think I don't care about them" will only diminish your ability to connect with the group and speak honestly.

Present the plain facts. Without editorializing or being overly dramatic, explain the situation as clearly and concisely as possible. For example: Saying "Last quarter our sales were down by 27 percent" is better than "Last quarter our sales really sucked and plummeted a gigantic 27 percent!" Offer an overview of what caused the situation and the measures that will be taken as a result. Outline who will be affected and the timing involved.

Be caring but not overly emotional. As you present the facts of the situation, you may feel yourself getting sad, disappointed, or angry. Getting swallowed up in your personal feelings can fan the emotional flames of the audience and lead to an out-of-control gripe session. For example: "I know this is hard, but some of you will have the option of relocating to the new headquarters" is better than "For some reason *they* decided to move headquarters—which really chaps my hide—and some of you will unfairly end up there."

Provide follow-up resources. Always leave at least a few minutes at the end of your presentation for questions. In addition, consider setting up a Website specifically designed to address the common concerns and/or provide a designated human resources person for fielding calls. If layoffs are inevitable, consider providing outplacement seminars and resources for those affected.

Drop the jokes. Starting with a joke or humorous icebreaker in the face of bad news is usually inappropriate. Trying to sugarcoat a distasteful subject will backfire and does nothing but exacerbate the stress that your audience already feels.

Introduce Speakers With Confidence

You've heard the old joke "there's nothing like a great introduction, and that was *nothing* like a great introduction." The ability to confidently present a speaker is an important professional skill to possess.

Why even bother with a preamble? you might wonder. *Wouldn't it be more efficient to just let the presenter get up and start pontificating?* Not really. A good introduction is like a warm-up act for a rock star. It gives the audience time to settle in, focuses their attention, creates anticipation, and in general sets the stage for a great performance.

Poor introductions can have the opposite impact and put an audience to sleep before the speaker has even stepped onto the platform. A well-worked-out introduction answers three fundamental questions:

- Why are we here?
- Who is the speaker?
- What will they be talking about?

Speaker Savvy: Be sure to talk to both the conference chairperson and the speaker in preparing your talk. The conference chair can help you understand the main points to get across to the audience and the speaker can provide you with specific details on their credentials, speech title, and content.

Once you have done your research and know what you want to say, you're ready to write. A good basic format includes an opening, body, and wrap-up. Consider the following example:

Opening: "Good morning. My name is Jim Worrywart; I am the vice president of Crisis International. I have the privilege of introducing today's speaker. As you all know, we have been facing some challenges in the past six months here at CI, due to the devaluation of the dollar around the world."

Body: "Our speaker today is a recognized expert in the area of global crisis. She has been written about in *Time, Newsweek,* and *Fortune* magazine. She is a regular commentator on the popular news show *Things Can Always Get Worse* and the author of the best-selling book *It's Really Not a Crisis After All.* Today she is going to speak to us about how our company can weather the storm and come out as survivors."

Wrap-up: "I invite you to sit back and enjoy today's presentation— *How to Make Mountains Out of Molehills.* Please join me in welcoming Hedda Tohellwithit."

Introduction Cheat Sheet

Do's	Dont's
Practice ahead of time.	Wing it.
Know the exact pronunciation of the speaker's name.	Guess how he/she says it.
Know the speaker's exact title or position.	Presume his/her position.
Be brief and to the point (3 minutes max).	Take time away from the speaker with a long introduction.
Use notes sparingly.	Read your entire introduction.
Introduce yourself.	Assume everyone knows who you are.
Be lively and enthusiastic.	Act like you were forced to do this.
Take a moment or two before you begin to speak.	Rush into talking before you are ready.
Wait at the podium and shake the speaker's hand.	Rush off as soon as you're done.
Use humor very sparingly and only if appropriate.	Tell a cheesy joke.

Hire the Right Speaker

The most enthusiastic, energetic speaker in the world won't do you much good if he/she mostly talks to attorneys and your audience is a group of farmers who want to hear about the latest developments in wheat whacking machinery. Likewise, the most learned speaker, who is a yawn to listen to, won't be as well received as a lively talker with a good take on the topic. If you're only one of the key speakers at your company's next event, but still bear the responsibility of choosing who will share the platform with you, the following quick pick checklist can help narrow the field down to a few choice candidates.

For each question, give yourself the following:

0 points if your answer is "not at all"

1 point if your answer is "to a small degree"

2 points if your answer is "to a moderate degree"

3 points if your answer is "to a large degree"

1. How well does the speaker's topic fit my audience's need? _____

2. In watching the speaker's video or seeing his/her live performance, how good a job does the speaker do at *entertaining* the audience?_____

3. In watching the speaker's video or seeing his/her live performance, how good a job does the speaker do at *educating* the audience?_____

4. In watching the speaker's video or seeing his/her live performance, how good a job does the speaker do at *engaging* the audience's participation?_____

5. In watching the speaker's video or seeing his/her live performance, how good a job does the speaker do at using *appropriate humor*?_____

6. To what degree does the speaker do pre-event research and customize the program based on what he/she discovers?_____

7. Does the speaker use adequate audiovisual materials or handouts?_____

8. Is the speaker willing and able to be accessible to the audience for questions and comments both before and after the event? _____

9. Does the speaker seem easy to work with and responsive to our needs and requests? _____

10. Were the references contacted satisfied with the services the speaker provided?_____

Total Score:_____

26–30 points: Congratulations—you have a winner. This person will more than likely hit a home run with your group. If you can't afford his/her fee, try to negotiate by offering to promote his/her book, provide him/her with marketing lists, or other incentives.

13–25 points: This person has quite a few of the qualities you are looking for in a speaker, and would be an adequate choice if he/she fits your budget.

0–12 points: Unless you are desperate—or this is all you can afford—pass on this speaker. He/she won't meet your needs or satisfy your audience.

Look Beyond Topic

When reviewing a potential speaker's demonstration tape, don't get stuck on the content or topic of the talk itself. Remember that presentation was customized for that client. Instead, focus on the person's skill as a presenter. How good a job did he/she do at entertaining, educating, and engaging the audience?

Sparkle on the TV

"Lights, camera, action!" Television interviews can be a little daunting—all those hundreds of thousands of people watching you—but they also provide some of the best PR exposure you can get. If you have the opportunity to be interviewed on television, this list of do's and don'ts will help you to have a successful on-screen appearance.

Do's	Dont's
Choose what you wear carefully. Women should wear bright, solid colors; men should wear a dark suit or jacket and light-colored shirt.	Wear white, black, large patterns, or flashy jewelry. In general, these do not translate well over the air.
Arrive early and meet the producer. Discuss any last-minute angles or ideas he/she may have.	Show up at the last minute without having time to orient yourself to the studio and staff.
Bring your book or any other materials you are promoting. Give these, your Website, and contact details to the producer when you arrive so that they can be put on screen if appropriate.	Be shy about using the TV opportunity to leverage your products or services but also don't make your on-screen appearance a thinly veiled commercial.
Use facial expressions and hand gestures to animate your presentation.	Overdo gestures. TV is a medium where small comes off really big.
Sit upright, leaning forward slightly.	Slouch.
Prepare three or four short and concise key points that you want to make during the interview.	Get sidetracked, lose your focus, and make long-winded points.
Talk to and look at the interviewer when answering his/her questions.	Be surprised or derailed if the interviewer (off camera) checks his/her notes and pays no attention to you. Also, don't look at the camera, unless instructed to do so by the interviewer.
Know the format and audience of the program. If possible, watch a few episodes of the show before you go on.	Deliver your message to an audience you haven't identified or thought about.
Prepare your answers so that they are no longer than 30 seconds.	Keep talking to the point where the interviewer has to interrupt you.
Assume that you will be on camera all the time and act accordingly.	Make any gestures or mannerisms that you don't want broadcast!
Explain things simply and concisely. Use language that is easy for everyone to understand.	Use technical jargon or "in-house" terms that will not be understood by everyone.

Shine on the Radio

Radio interviews are a challenging form of public speaking because you don't see your audience. In most cases, they take the form of interviews conducted over the phone by the host of the show who asks you questions about your subject of expertise. Your radio experience will be even more fun for you (and informative for your audience) if you follow these guidelines:

Find Out Who's Calling Whom

Will the radio station be calling you, or are they expecting you to call them? Nothing will throw you off your game like the last-minute panic of not knowing who's calling whom, just before you are supposed to go on air. If they are making contact with you, be sure to provide them with the phone number where you can be reached on the date and time of the interview. If you are calling them, get both the call-in number and the studio number in case of emergency.

Speaker Savvy: *Get the producer's name and direct-dial phone number. If for any reason you cannot make the interview, or you need to change your interview phone number, the person to talk to is the show's producer.*

Sound Awake

Many radio talk shows take place during commute times, so if you are on the West Coast and they the East, you will likely be spouting your pearls of wisdom at 4 or 5 a.m. Don't plan on just rolling out of bed, reaching for the phone, and giving a brilliant radio interview—you will sound groggy and unfocused. Instead, get up with enough time to shake off your sleepy voice, rev up your brain cells, and go give those New England motorists a morning they won't soon forget.

Get a Time Line

Most radio interviews are brief, lasting no more than 10 or 15 minutes. In this situation, the host is looking for short sound bites that he or she can use for making a comment or asking a question. Long-winded explanations and lots of detail are not the stuff of great, pithy radio interviews. On the other hand, if your segment is scheduled to last for 30 minutes to an hour, you have the room to go into more depth with your answers and tell stories to illustrate your point. The key is to be substantive, in short sentences.

Prepare Your Main Points

If you are being interviewed about a book you have written, then have the book in front of you for reference while on air. Tag any pages or parts that you particularly want to cover or that are pertinent to the topic being discussed. If not, prepare a list of any tips, facts, figures, and examples you want to cover, and keep them in front of you during the interview. Beware: Regardless of the scheduled topic, once the interview begins, you may find that the host goes off on a topical tangent, so be prepared to cover the full range of your subject.

Accept Being the Straight Man (or Woman)

Interviews conducted by a comedian (or hosts who think they are) can be challenging if the focus is more on cracking jokes than listening to what you have to say. If your answers become the launching pad for gags, then graciously surrender to the fate of being the straight man. Don't attempt to be funny in return and upstage your interviewer. It usually doesn't work—and sounds pathetic. Simply put your ego out to dry and laugh along.

Know the Station's Target Audience

Ask the producer in a pre-interview phone call who the listeners are. For example: If the show airs in the middle of the day, there's a good possibility that stay-at-home moms listen in. The examples you would craft for this demographic are dramatically different than those for a radio show with an audience of teenagers. Producers and radio hosts love guests who can speak to the needs, concerns, interests, and desires of their audience.

Give Good Answers to Silly Questions

If the interviewer asks you a question that you find difficult to answer, such as *"I was put on hold for 10 minutes yesterday; what's wrong with people?"* instead of answering the question directly, make a leap to the subject you want to talk about. (Hint: You see politicians do this all time.) For example: If your expertise is telephone etiquette, you can say, *"I know it can be frustrating when you get poor service. I have found that many service people are never trained in basic telephone etiquette. What I always recommend is...."*

Plan Your Teleclass in Advance

With the rising cost of travel, live classroom training has become an expensive proposition that often leaves small and medium-sized businesses scratching their heads as to how to provide employee education in a cost-effective and efficient way. Enter the teleclass—a telephone classroom that offers an inexpensive and convenient alternative. Because of the obvious (and not so obvious) differences between telephone and face-to-face trainings, it's good business to plan ahead for the best way to package and present your material over the phone.

The first question to consider is the length of your program. Think hours here instead of days. Your best bet is a session time of between one and two hours. A one-hour teleclass allows you to deliver the basic information and take a few questions. A two-hour teleclass leaves additional room for exercises and group comments. If the content you want to deliver will take longer, consider doing a session a week, over a two- to four-week time period.

Next, determine how many people you are going to train at one time. The technology you use will factor strongly into this decision. For example: The usual method of participant connection is through a bridge, which accommodates between 25 and 30 callers at one time. More callers can often be added, but the price increases. The other factor is your comfort level. How big a group would you be at ease with? Keep in mind that, the fewer the attendees, the more time and attention you can spend on individual questions, comments, and needs.

Speaker Savvy: *If you've ever had a phone call where you tried to patch in a third person, you know how quickly the sound deteriorates. Using a company that specializes in telephone bridges removes this problem and provides clear reception for all your participants because the company provides a central number to call into. Some companies, such as* www.mrconference.com, *provide a free service; others, such as* www.telephonebridgeservices.com, *charge by the hour. If you want to record your teleclass, look for companies that offer this feature with their package.*

Even though the main delivery of the content will take place over the phone, your teleclass will be more informative and interesting if your group has support materials such as diagrams, graphs, and data to focus on while you talk. Decide what support materials you want to provide and how you are going to deliver them. For example: PDF files are a simple way of e-mailing materials that display on most computers. To avoid distraction while on the call, you can request that participants print out a hard copy ahead of time. Alternatively, you can place all materials on a Website that the participants access simultaneously while on the call. Doing this transforms your teleclass into a seminar on the Web, otherwise known as a Webinar.

Lastly, you need to set up a simple and easy method for the participants to register and, if appropriate, pay for the teleclass. The easiest method for registration is e-mail. People write to request a spot in the class and you respond with a confirmation that includes the session time, date, instructions on how to access the teleclass, an overview of what will be covered, and any prework assigned. If you plan on charging for the teleclass, using a service such as PayPal or CCNow will relieve you of having to set up a credit card account with your bank.

> ### Better Late Than Never
> Just as it is with live training, you will usually have one or two people join your teleclass while it is already in session. Clearly it's inappropriate to stop the class in order to bring a latecomer up to speed. The best alternative is to record the class and then offer the audio track to all attendees at no additional charge. This is especially useful when conducting a series where there's a high chance that some people will miss some sessions.

Lead a Top-Notch Teleclass

Aware of it or not, you pick up visual cues from the people around you. A smile might tell you that your coworker is happy, a frown that your boss is having a bad day! According to research conducted by Professor Albert Mehrabian at UCLA, 55 percent of the perceptions we have about others we receive from their body language, 38 percent from their tone of voice, and only 7 percent from the words they use.

Unfortunately, when you're tasked with leading a teleclass, more than half of your presentation punch is lost in translation. Here are five tips for breaking the sound barrier and creating audience rapport:

Avoid Information Overload

Though you may have the material that you are delivering down cold, your audience is probably hearing it for the first time, and what can seem like a straightforward summary to you, might feel overwhelming to them. You can avoid giving people too much information, too quickly, by covering no more than eight to 10 key points during a two-hour teleclass (less for a 60- or 90-minute session).

Leave Room for Silence

Novice teleclass leaders sometimes feel uneasy when they pose a question and hear a big loud nothing at the other end of the line. Relax. Remember that people need time to absorb what you have said, and short periods of silence allow students to gather their thoughts and reflect. Also, you can use silence to stress an important point you have just made by staying quiet for a few seconds afterward.

Encourage Questions

Don't panic if, on paper, your teleclass overview looks as if it could be delivered in 30 minutes rather than the scheduled 60. Because a vital component of a successful session is participation, rather than talk your audience into oblivion, plan on stopping every 10 to 15 minutes and asking them if they have any questions or comments. Regularly checking in allows you to "read" what is going on with them, even though you are "working blind."

Reach Out

Each person attending the teleclass will participate to different degrees. There are always those people who will pipe up right from the start and those who won't say a word. To even out the participation, keep a list of class participants in front of you as you lead the course and make notes about who has spoken and who hasn't. Reach out by asking a specific class member, who has not yet shared, to make a comment or ask a question.

Stay on Track

Don't lose your focus—and your audience—by spending too much time on questions or comments that are not within the scope of your teleclass. If a simple answer doesn't suffice and if it looks as if the conversation is headed down a rabbit hole with no light at the end, politely suggest the participant e-mail you for further clarification. Keeping one person happy at the expense of the group is a teleclass no-no.

Set Up a Teleconference

As part of your presenter preparation, you may find yourself wanting to set up a teleconference with the meeting planner and key players to discuss the upcoming event. The success of the call rests on your shoulders, so little up-front effort will ensure an efficient and effective call:

Schedule a time that works across zones. Check on the locations of all attendees and pick a time that is reasonable for everyone. Four p.m. Pacific may be a convenient time for you to participate in a teleconference, but it probably won't be such a joy for anyone located on the East Coast (7 p.m.) and—worse still—a real bust with those participants located in the London office (midnight)! If you have to schedule a call outside of normal business hours, check with the folks in that area to see which end of the spectrum (earlier or later) would work best for them.

Send an agenda prior to the call. At least 24 hours before the call, notify attendees of the conference call telephone number, the passcode (if you are using an audio conferencing service), the exact time of the call *in their time zone,* and an agenda that specifies the purpose of the call, topics to be discussed, and names of those who will be leading and participating on the call. If any handouts or reading material is necessary, send it out at least 24–48 hours prior to the teleconference.

Speaker Savvy: As a backup, provide your name and cell phone number in case any callers have trouble connecting.

Set up a cell phone protocol. More than likely some of your teleconference attendees will be calling in from a cell phone. If their call is disconnected (because they drove through a tunnel or walked past a hairpin), set up clear protocols in advance about how to rejoin the meeting already in progress.

Consider recording the meeting. Because it's inevitable that at least a few people will miss some or all of the teleconference, it's smart time management to record the call and make the mp3 file available to all attendees via e-mail. Alternatively, there are audio conferencing services that, for a small fee, will record the call and allow members who missed out to dial in and listen at their own convenience.

Invest in a good headset. To ensure freedom of movement (and to prevent you from getting a cramped neck), be sure to have a top quality headset on hand. Companies such as Plantronics (*www.plantronics.com*) and Logitech (*www.logitech.com*) feature different styles and a range of prices.

Take Advantage of Teleconference Technology

For the economy-minded business (and who isn't these days?) a teleconference provides an inexpensive way to gather a geographically diverse group together to discuss ideas. Using the telephone as a virtual meeting room is cost effective and efficient if you as the fearless teleconference leader follow these simple guidelines for conducting the call:

Start on Time

Don't make the punctual people hang around on the other end of the line waiting for the latecomers to join in. If you need to buy a little time, start with roll call and introductions so that everyone knows who is on the call and you know whom you are still waiting for.

Review Teleconference Etiquette

Hidden behind the safety of the telephone, people will be tempted to fidget and fiddle while on the call. They may be checking their e-mail, calling into their cell phone voice mail, writing a quick memo, playing online poker, or watching the weather report in Bora Bora. Regardless, such distractions (and the little keyboard clicking sounds that accompany them) can steal your focus and others away from the topic of the call. Before jumping into the heart of your topic, review basic teleconference etiquette such as:

- Avoid putting your phone on hold if it has a "music on hold" feature. Instead, to prevent background noise from disturbing the group, use the mute button when you are not speaking, but remember to un-mute when you want to talk.
- If possible, turn off your call waiting to avoid the interruption beep being heard by everyone else on the call.
- Avoid using the speakerphone, as it will pick up background noise.
- Don't answer e-mail, surf the Net, or do any other activity that makes noise or takes your attention during the call.

Take Breaks

If your teleconference is scheduled to go longer than two hours, take a five- to 10-minute bio-break every 60–90 minutes. Instead of having participants hang up and call back (a potential logistical nightmare), just have them put the phone on mute until they return.

Manage Questions and Comments

Don't assume that a teleconference requires less crowd control than a face-to-face meeting. For example: Because you won't be able to see the participants raise their hands when they have a question or comment, set up a protocol for discussions at the beginning of the call. The best bet for a teleconference is to stop at the end of each section or main point and inquire if anyone in the group has anything to say. Ask the participants to state their name and location first before beginning. For example: *"Hi. This is Jeff Goldstone from Georgia. My question is...."*

Ensure a Balanced Discussion

As the teleconference progresses, keep a note of those people who have spoken and those who haven't. If appropriate, invite those people yet to voice an opinion to participate. For example: *"Cindy, in Albuqueque, any thoughts on this?"*

Ask Questions of Individuals

Instead of asking questions to the group at large, which can cause confusion, pose your questions to individuals. If you want to ask a question of the entire group, ask each person to write down his/her answer first and then open the floor for general discussion.

Address Distractions

If background noise is interfering with the call, gently reinfore the guidelines you set at the beginning. For example: Say, *"I'm hearing a lot of background noise it sounds like...a dog barking; the clacking of a keyboard; the whirl of a blender making margaritas! It's becoming distracting, so please keep the noise to a minimum until we finish the call."*

End on an Action Note

Bring proper closure to the call by thanking everyone for participating, reviewing action items discussed, and confirming any scheduled follow-up meetings.

Facilitate a Videoconference

Videoconferencing is a great tool for groups who want to attend a speaking engagement at the same time, but are located in different places. For example: A team in Chicago, their counterparts in the Philippines, and the project leaders in the UK all might want to "meet" electronically and discuss research developments.

At each location, a camera operator videos the actions of the group, who are usually seated around three sides of a conference table. When a partcipant takes the floor, the cameraperson zooms in for a close-up shot of the person speaking. Each location watches the action on a video screen that shows the other two groups. The result is that everyone can see and hear everyone else.

As you can imagine, being the facilitator or presenter for such a setup demands that you understand (and manage) a few critical success factors:

Technology

Successful videoconferences rest on the technology they employ. The odds are that, the more equipment involved in the electronic linkup, the more likely there will be a technical glitch. You can help eliminate last-minute problems by giving yourself enough time to become familiar with the setup and checking well in advance that *everything* is working. Keep in mind that if there are problems during the actual meeting, and you don't have technical assistance available, the facilitator (you) is the one responsible for working with the video operations people to fix any problems.

Visual Aids

Oftentimes groups will be in a facility where the television monitor they are watching is much smaller than the standard overhead screen. PowerPoint presentations should be adapted for the confined screen by placing less information on each slide, and using shorter sentences and a larger font size.

Also, using clear, large, high-contrast graphics will aid readability when transmitted.

Sound Control

In a normal meeting, quiet side conversations cause minimal disruption, but during a videoconference, microphones easily pick up such distracting sounds and even amplify them. To avoid this ask everyone to mute their microphones when they are not speaking on air. This will also minimize background noise.

> ### Put a Protocol in Place
> Set up a protocol for asking questions and making comments. For example: If a UK team member has a question for someone in the Chicago group, should he/she interrupt, raise his/her hand, and wait to be called on, or will there be a specific time set aside for asking questions? Additionally, ask the group leaders at all locations to repeat questions asked by their team so that everyone can hear.

Beware the Mood Makers

According to Merriam-Webster, *mood* is defined as *a prevailing attitude; a receptive state of mind predisposing to action; and a distinctive atmosphere or context.* The question is: What can you do as a speaker to set or shift the mood of your audience so that they are as responsive as possible to what you have to offer? Here are some common mood makers and what you can do about them:

Mood Maker: Mandatory attendance. If the group has been forced to attend your training, speech, or presentation (especially as punishment for recent poor performance), they will, at best, be disinterested and, at worst, downright resentful and hostile.

Mood Breaker: The key in this situation is to get your audience participating (and laughing) as soon as possible. This can be achieved by doing a humorous, pertinent role-play with a volunteer from the audience, setting up a small-group exercise or paired sharing, or inviting them to ask questions right from the start. You want to give the group the message that you are on their side and are going to do your best to make this time fun *and* valuable for them.

Mood Maker: Following a boring speaker. If you are unfortunate enough to speak after a monotonous, lackluster presenter, you may have to dig your audience out of a deep hole of boredom.

Mood Breaker: You can immediately set a new tone by being extra-expressive the moment you step on stage. Exaggerate your voice and gestures to grab the audience's attention and signal that you, unlike your predecessor, will be an interesting speaker to listen to. In an emergency situation, give them a quick stretch break so you can quickly get them back to the land of the living.

Mood Maker: Afternoon energy crash. Have you ever noticed that when people get back from lunch or afternoon break, their energy levels often drop like a stone? High-carbohydrate, sugary, calorie-laden foods (such as cookies, brownies, and cake) are often the culprit.

Mood Breaker: If you are speaking to a group in the latter part of the day, ask the event coordinator to switch out the afternoon break sweets for fresh fruit, mixed nuts, cheese, or raw vegetables. You can also try serving lunch on the late side (around 1 p.m.). This makes the afternoon session, when people are the sleepiest, a bit shorter.

Mood Maker: Uneven participation. Left to their own devices, people will often gravitate toward the part of the room that reflects their mood. For example: The front section is filled with people who are ready and willing to learn, the back rows are packed with doubters who need to ensure a quick getaway, and the side sections are occupied by people who are uncertain and undecided about the session.

Mood Breaker: By moving people around for an exercise or other group activity, you break up the default seating pattern and get more participation from more of the group. Also be sure to direct points and questions—even rhetorical ones—to various parts of the room. Don't fall into the trap of playing to the favorable front rows.

Overcome the Unplanned

Sooner or later, every speaker will face unexpected, unplanned for, and unwelcome situations they will have to deal with. Veteran presenters have learned that dealing with breakdowns is part and parcel of the game. However, for less-seasoned speakers, these changes can threaten to undermine their confidence and delivery. The following lists some not-as-unusual-as-you-might-expect scenarios and what to do about them.

Scenario	What to Do About It
You're feeling sick before the presentation.	Though you don't need to be a martyr if you are really too sick to get out of bed, or if doing so would endanger your health, most speakers still follow "the show must go on" credo.If you're fighting a cold, flu, or fever, dose yourself up with whatever your doctor suggests will get you through the talk. It's always a good idea to travel with over-the-counter medications, such as a pain reliever and decongestant, but beware of anything that might make you drowsy. If proceeding with your presentation is impossible or would be detrimental, apologize to the organizer and provide them with several recommendations for substitute speakers they can call on.
The previous speaker runs overtime.	This happens more often than you think, so it's always a good idea to have plan B ready to go. Be prepared by figuring out beforehand what topics from your talk can be cut or drastically shortened. Often, by removing an exercise or role-play, you can save a chunk of time. Resist the temptation to make a remark about the previous speaker's sloppy time management. This won't buy back any time, but will make you look like an unprofessional crybaby.

Your talk goes on longer than expected and you run out of time.	To avoid this situation in the first place, have a clock (other than your watch) clearly visible and use a helper at the back of the room to signal you at specific time cues such as 15, 10, and five minutes to go. A word of advice: Checking you wristwatch will give the impression that you can't wait to get out of there. Prior to going live, prepare a time line of your talk based upon a few run-throughs. Have a start and end time for each part, and frequently check to make sure you're on track. If you find that you are running behind, cut out some material. The audiences won't know what they are missing and you can keep everyone happy by ending on time. If possible, use the Q&A to cover some of the content you had to lose along the way.
You notice typos in your materials.	An ounce of prevention is worth a pound of cure, so always use your computer's spellchecker and then have a human spellchecker look over the material before you print or dispatch it Even with rigorous quality control, typos can mystically appear once you have gone to print. If this happens during your presentation, a simple acknowledgment such as, "I just noticed a typo on page 8; my apologies for that" will usually handle the situation. Some speakers even make a game of it and say, "I just want to do a test and see how detail-oriented this group is: There is a typo on page 8. Can anyone find it?"
The audience is much smaller than you expected.	Be aware that sometimes, for no obvious reason, your talk will be attended by far fewer the number of people than you (or the organizers) expected. When the audience is considerably smaller, it can feel like a blow to the ego, so beware of getting stuck in thoughts such as *I'm obviously not a speaker they want to hear* or *this is clearly not a popular topic*. These can hinder your delivery and hamper your enthusiasm. Instead, re-adjust your presentation for the small audience you have. Consider moving people closer to the front of the room so the group is less scattered and more unified. A smaller group affords you the opportunity to build rapport through more in-depth dialogue.

Take on Technical Breakdowns

No matter how well you practice and plan your presentation, if Mercury is in retrograde, all sorts of bothersome technical glitches can threaten to unravel your stellar speech. Following is a list of common technical difficulties and some smart ways of dealing with them:

Scenario	What to Do About It
Your slide show doesn't work.	To prevent the problem of your cable not fitting into their equipment (or vice versa), travel with an adapter that ensures compatibility no matter what technology your host provides. Most seasoned speakers will travel with a copy (on CD or USB flash drive) of their slideshow so that it can be loaded onto the host's computer if there are any connectivity issues. In the worst case they can be printed up as handouts. If you are one of many speakers in a lineup, don't assume your slideshow will work when you get on stage. Be safe and plan an earlier time for testing your equipment and making sure *your* slideshow is working. As a final standby, if all else fails, carry hard copies of your slides that can be duplicated and given to the attendees during or after your talk.
Your handouts don't arrive.	As above, carry a spare set in hardcopy and on CD so that they can be copied on site and distributed to the audience.
Your microphone malfunctions.	If you have a large audience where amplification is essential, make certain there is a hooked-up, working, backup microphone close at hand—before you begin your speech. If the mic fails during your talk, and there is no backup, apologize and have

	your audience do an exercise or role-play while the techies fix the problem. If the room is relatively small, speak without a microphone until the problem is fixed.
The fire alarm goes off during your talk.	Although it's comforting to know that most fire alarms are false alarms, you must take the signal seriously and prepare to evacuate the room. Your audience will be concerned, so act calmly and reassure them that you will find out if an evacuation of the building is necessary. (Assign an assistant to do this.) While you are waiting for confirmation, locate exits and fire extinguisher locations. If the alarm is false then continue your presentation with a light-hearted remark ("I must be on fire today") to relieve the tension. If the alarm is real, don't rush off the stage, but instruct the participants how to evacuate the room using all available exits.
The room is too hot or too cold.	If your presentation is taking place in a hotel or conference facility, get the contact number of the person responsible for thermostat control (usually the banquet manager) before your talk. Arrive in the room at least 30 minutes before the start of your talk so that you can adjust the temperature accordingly (remember the temperature will go up a few degrees once the room is filled with warm bodies).
The room is set up badly.	Whenever possible send a room setup diagram to the facility before the event. Include approximate measurements of aisles, and so forth. If, when you arrive in the room, the setup is too bad to live with, ask for it to be changed to a better configuration. If the problem is the shape of the room (for example, it is very wide and not very deep), apologize to your audience and invite those seated at the far ends to move if they need to. Ditto for a pillar that obstructs the audience's view.

Stop Ramblers in Their Tracks

Part of the challenge of presenting, especially in meetings and other small forums, is balancing good listening skills with time efficiency. If you're not careful, ramblers can easily derail you by going on and on long after their point has been made or their question asked. Waiting around for the conversation to get back on track takes up valuable time and irritates the other audience members. Bridging is a three-part technique for politely steering the conversation back in the direction you want it to go in, while at the same time retaining rapport with the rambler.

Step 1: Catch them breathing.

Bridging requires you to interrupt audience members. Although that may sound rude, it doesn't have to be, if you simply wait for them to take a breath. If an audience member is excited or speaking quickly, you may have to listen more intently, but it's a guarantee he/she will eventually take a breath. When he/she does, a short gap will occur in the conversation. That's when you seize the moment to interrupt.

Step 2: Validate and acknowledge the audience member.

Validating and acknowledging what the audience member has just said softens the abruptness of cutting into the conversation. For example: Imagine you are presenting the monthly sales report to a group of department heads throughout your company when your fellow executive from accounting starts to get way off base on a rant about company policy and his dog. He says, *"I want the policies mailed to my work address. The last time policies were mailed to my home, the dog got to them before I did, and they were shredded out of existence. She's a poodle, and they're not usually aggressive, but when she hears the mailman, she turns into a monster. I used to have a St. Bernard, and he could've taken the door off if he'd wanted to...."*

Heard enough? Okay. Wait for the breath and then use one of the validation and acknowledgement statements that follow. For example: *"I can see why you want them mailed to the office."* Then move on to Step 3.

Validation Statements

I understand what you are saying.

I can see why you would feel that way.

Thank you for sharing that.

Let me ask you a question about what you just said.

I can see how....

That's a good point.

Many people feel that way.

I'm glad that you brought that up.

Step 3: Redirect the conversation.

Having interrupted with validation, the last part of bridging is steering the conversation back in the direction you want it to go. Some of the best ways to redirect the conversation are by asking a question, making a strong statement, or offering an opinion. Continuing the chewed-policy example, redirecting the conversation may sound like this: *"I can see how not receiving your policies would be a big inconvenience. I'll make sure the policies are mailed to your business, but first I want to finish going over the new limits of the policy."*

Address Audience Participation Problems

Most audiences are well behaved and appreciative, and want to see you succeed. Now and again you might find yourself in a situation where this isn't the case. Some common examples are:

- If attendance is mandatory, your audience may be a bit moody.
- If you are discussing an inflammatory subject, your audience may be up in arms.
- If your audience is burned out, overworked, or just plum tuckered, they may sit there like lumps on a log.

The following list offers some tried-and-true ways of dealing with common audience issues:

Scenario	What to Do About It
Your audience doesn't want to be there.	This can be off-putting for a speaker, but the best strategy is not to focus on the mood in the room but continue on with as much enthusiasm as you can muster. On no account mention the resistant attitude that you notice, because any conversation about it will be slow death—for you! Close to the beginning of your talk, have attendees introduce themselves (to either the whole group or someone seated next to them) and say what they do at work. You'll be surprised how a little participation can quickly shift the mood. In your introduction make a point of telling them what, in your presentation, will be useful for them and why.

The audience doesn't ask questions.	If your talk was particularly engrossing, it may take a while for your audience to gather themselves together and get into question-asking mode. If, after giving them some time to ask questions, they still don't have any, then prime the pump by saying, "A question that I get asked a lot is...."Alternatively, ask people to write down one question they have and then divide them into small groups to discuss the questions. At the end, ask if any group has a question that they would like to share with the whole room.
Audience members arrive late.	If the late arrivals show up within five minutes of starting your talk, take a moment to welcome them and ensure that they have the appropriate handout materials. If people arrive halfway through a presentation—and you have a small audience—greet them courteously and talk to them on a break, just to check in. If the whole room arrives late (which can happen at tightly scheduled conferences), consider cutting something out of your talk so that you can still end at the published time.
People come back late from the breaks.	To help prevent this from happening, set up your breaks so that everyone is clear about timing. Say something like, "In a moment we are going to take a break. We have a lot of material to cover, so I would appreciate it if everyone would get back into the room, in their seats, ready to begin, by 10:45." It speeds up the break process for people if you point out beverage stations, give directions to rest rooms, and suggest that they not get too hung up with cell phones or e-mail until the longer meal break coming up later on.
Your audience is having a post-lunch slump.	The sugar in the dessert is usually the culprit that sends people to slumberland 15 minutes into the afternoon session. If you have any control over the menu, ask that fruit be served for dessert instead of the customary cheesecake. Plan on an active after-lunch kickoff. Get people moving by doing exercises, role-plays, discussion groups, or anything participative that will them help shake off the snoozes.

Your audience is angry.	Don't take sides. Instead, present in a positive way that you understand their anger and frustration. Don't add fuel to their fire, but rather express the type of empathy that says "I hear you." Break them up into pairs or small groups and ask them to brainstorm solutions to the problem or situation they are upset about. Then have a general group sharing about the solutions they came up with. Make them laugh. Even for the most riled up groups it's hard to stay angry in the face of giggles and guffaws.

Dueling Discussions

Valuable time is often eaten up in meetings, trainings, seminars, and small-group speeches by a dueling discussion. This is when two people, or two groups of people, have opposing ideas and the group is stalled by deadlock. If this happens on your watch do one or all of the following:

- Ask a question that directs attention away from the deadlock and has both parties take a breath as they consider the answer.

- Choose a participant who is not engaged in the argument and ask what he/she thinks about the situation. Say something like, "Gayle, you are sitting there listening intently, what are your thoughts about this issue?"

- Interrupt the "dueling" by saying something like, "I know that you both have strong opinions about this, but I'd like to open up the conversation to the group and give someone who hasn't yet said anything the chance to talk."

Borrow From the Best

As the saying goes, "God is in the details." Here's a roundup of what some of the best trainers, speakers, and presenters in the business say about the small, easy-to-miss details that make a good presentation, great. Simple to implement, they work like a charm to gain audience participation and engagement.

- If you are leading a group discussion and want it to continue, say, "What else?" If you want to bring the discussion to a close, say, "Anything else?"

- After answering any question, no matter how small or complex, confirm the listener's satisfaction by asking, "Does that answer your question?" This reinforces your commitment to listening and responding to the group's questions.

- To get an audience to raise their hands in response to a question, create a physical anchor by raising your hand while you simultaneously say, "Please raise your hands if...."

- When you ask a question of a group, expect a few moments of silence while they figure out their answers. Don't jump in and, in a panic, start talking. If you still don't get a response after 30 seconds or so, try asking the same question but in a different way.

- Although you can always ask the group if anyone has a question, wants to share, or is willing to assist you in an exercise, don't be afraid to volunteer specific people as well. As long as you give them the room to decline, asking an individual to participate sets a healthy tone of participation.

- Don't get stuck focusing on one part of the classroom (the front left-hand side, for example) or a few highly participative individuals. Instead, work the room in a clockwise and counterclockwise pattern by choosing people to participate from each area of the room— front left, back left, front right, back right, and middle.

- While you're talking and delivering information, scan the room in a W pattern to make eye contact with as many different people as possible.

- If you are going to walk from stage right to stage left, stride forth with confidence. Walking with purpose, as opposed to wandering aimlessly or distractedly out of nervousness, adds power to your presentation. If you are making a particular point, to a particular participant, move in his/her general direction.

- If a particular participant gets off on a tangent, rant, or long-winded story, build a bridge to bring him/her back. Wait for him/her to take a breath, and politely interrupt by saying, "I think I understand what you are talking about" or "I hear what you are saying" and then connect back to a point related to the material.

- Especially when conducting classroom trainings or meetings, whenever possible, use the whole space of the stage or front of the room to move about. Don't hide nervously behind a podium or table.

- Whenever you have paired sharing or small group discussions, always be sure to ask the participants to thank each other at the end of the exercise or dialogue.

- For every major point in your speech, tell the audience what you are going to tell them, then tell them what it is you want to tell them, and, finally, tell them what you told them. For example:

Tell them what you are going to tell them: *"Tonight I am going to talk about the exciting world of yak butter and all the delicious and nutritious recipes you can make at home...."*

Tell them what you want to tell them: *"Yak butter has been used for centuries to make a variety of delicious dishes. For example, has anyone here had yak butter scones? No? You have not lived until you've tried them...."*

Tell them you told them: *"We have talked about the health benefits of yak butter tonight, we discussed several daily uses, and you are going home with a recipe for yak butter ice cream...."*

- Place the participants in groups or pairs **before** you begin to give out instructions for a role-play or exercise. Then, set up and explain exercises and role-plays one step at a time. Giving out all the instructions at once will confuse even the smartest of audience members, lead to general chaos, and cause you to lose control of the room.
- Ask, "Does anyone need more time?" before ending and debriefing an exercise or role-play.

Conclusion

At the end of the day, any time you open your mouth to talk in front of other people, you are practicing the art of public speaking. If you're just at the beginning of your career as a presenter, give yourself a break. It takes time and experience to get to a level of ease and excellence. Old habits die hard, and new ones take a while to develop. Be patient with yourself. Pick one thing to work on and get good at it. Try not to compare yourself to those who have been doing it for 20 years!

If you are an old pro at public speaking, we don't need to tell you that there is always a new technique to learn, a bad habit to break, or a piece that could use some polish. Ask speakers you admire to listen to your presentations—live or on tape—and get their honest feedback. Don't be afraid to break out of your rut and try something new (even if what you have been doing is working), expand your horizons, and take a public speaking risk.

We hope the 60 ways presented in this book have helped you to feel more confident in your presentations, more relaxed when you have to talk in public, and more empowered to get your unique message across.

Index

Index

N

names, using audience
   members', 27
nervous energy, 73-74
nervousness and anxiety, 25
neutral language, 79

O

opposing viewpoints,
   addressing, 100
outline,
   creating an, 19-21
   sample, 20

P

panel moderator, being the, 108
panel, participating on a, 107-108
PowerPoint presentation, 49-50
presentation,
   details that make a great,
     141-143
   evaluate your, 53-56
   introduction to your, 25-27
public speaking, good, 15

Q

Q&A session, 46
   conducting a, 47-49
   defining a time for, 89
question, asking a key, 29
questionnaire to evaluate your
   presentation, 53-56
questions,
   application, 45
   big picture, 44-45
   closed-ended, 27
   meaning, 45
   recent findings, 30

rhetorical, 92
set up a microphone for, 92
"What About You?" 30
"What If?" 29-30
questions easy, making asking,
   46-47

R

radio interviews, 118-120
recent findings questions, 30
registration for your teleclass, 122
role-plays,
   debriefing, 44-45
   demonstrating, 39-42
   setting up, 42-44
room setup,
   formal, 87
   informal, 86-87

S

seating arrangements for
   medium-sized groups, 88
sensory language, 79-81
small-group savvy, practicing,
   86-87
speaker, hiring the right, 114-116
speakers, introducing, 112-113
speech, adjust the rate of your,
   70-71
stage fright, standing down, 59-60
statement, attention-grabbing, 28
statements, dramatic, 28
stories in your talk, using, 34-36
stories, inspirational, 99-100
story, composing a great, 37-39
storytelling, importance of, 35-36
sub-points for key points, 22-23
support materials for your
   teleclass, 121

About the Authors

Keith Bailey and Karen Leland are co-founders of Sterling Consulting Group, an international management consulting firm specializing in maximizing results through the people side of business. In business for 25 years, they have worked with more than 150,000 executives, managers, and front-line staff from a wide variety of industries, including retail, transportation, hospitality, high-tech, banking, and consumer goods.

Their consulting work in corporations and public speaking engagements have taken them throughout North America, Southeast Asia, Africa, and Europe. Their clients have included such companies as AT&T, American Express, Apple Computer, Avis Rent A Car, Bank of America, Bristol-Myers Squibb, DuPont, SC Johnson Wax, Lufthansa German Airlines, Microsoft, and Oracle, to name a few, as well as the British government.

In addition to their consulting work, Keith and Karen are sought-after experts by the media. They have been interviewed by dozens of newspapers, magazines, and television and radio stations, including the Associated Press International. *Time, Fortune, Newsweek, The New York Times, Entrepreneur Magazines, Ladies Home Journal, Self, Fitness,* CNN, *The Today Show,* and *Oprah.*

They are sought-after speakers and have presented for groups such as the Young Presidents Organization, the Society of Association Executives, the Society of Consumer Affairs, and the Direct Marketing Association.

Keith and Karen are the authors of five books, including three editions of the best-selling *Customer Service for Dummies* (Wiley Publishing), which has sold more than 200,000 copies and has been translated into Spanish, German, Korean, Chinese, and Polish, among other languages. In addition, they are the authors of *Watercolor Wisdom: How Smart People Prosper in the Face of Conflict, Pressure and Change* (New Harbinger, 2006); *Customer Service In An Instant: 60 Ways to Win Customers and Keep Them Coming Back* (Career Press, 2008); and *Time Management In An Instant: 60 Ways to Make the Most of Your Day* (Career Press, 2008).

Public Speaking
In An Instant

About Sterling Consulting Group

Sterling Consulting Group offers a variety of training programs, consulting, and keynote speeches. To learn more about our on-site training programs, or to book Karen or Keith to speak at your next event, please visit the Website at *www.scgtraining.com.* For any additional questions or to schedule an interview, contact Keith Bailey or Karen Leland at:

Sterling Consulting Group

180 Harbor Drive #208

Sausalito, CA 94965

(415) 331–5200

kleland@scgtraining.com

www.scgtraining.com

The
In An Instant
Series

Customer Service *In An Instant*
EAN 978-1-60163-013-1

E-Mail *In An Instant*
EAN 978-1-60163-017-9

Time Management *In An Instant*
EAN 978-1-60163-014-8

Visit *CareerPress.com* for more information.

To order call 1-800-227-3371 (in NJ 201-848-0310).

Business Essentials
From
Career Press

100 Ways to Motivate Others
How Great Leaders Can Produce
Insane Results Without Driving People Crazy
Steve Chandler
EAN 978-1-56414-771-4

6 Habits of Highly Effective Bosses
Stephen Kohn & Vincent O'Connell
EAN 978-1-56414-832-2

6 Habits of Highly Effective Teams
Stephen Kohn & Vincent O'Connell
EAN 978-1-56414-927-5

Ask the Right Questions, Hire the Best People
Ron Fry
EAN 978-1-56414-892-6

Bridging the Generation Gap
How to Get Radio Babies, Boomers, Gen Xers,
and Gen Yers to Work Together And Achieve More
Linda Gravett & Robin Throckmorton
EAN 978-1-56414-898-8

The Essential Supervisor's Handbook
A Quick and Handy Guide for Any Manager or Business Owner
Brette McWhorter Sember & Terrence Sember